HOSPITAL SKETCHES

by
Louisa May Alcott
(Author of *Little Women*)

A BLS PUBLICATION
Applewood Books

ISBN: 1-918222-78-8

Thank you for purchasing an Applewood Book. Applewood reprints America's lively classics—books from
the past which are still of interest to modern readers—
subjects such as cooking, gardening, money, travel,
nature, sports, and history. Applewood Books are dis-
tributed by The Globe Pequot Press of Old Saybrook,
CT. For a free copy of our current catalog, please write
to Applewood Books, c/o The Globe Pequot Press, Box
833, Old Saybrook, CT 06475-0833.

---

10 9 8 7 6 5

Library of Congress Cataloging-in-Publication Data
Alcott, Louisa May, 1832-1888.
     Hospital sketches / by Louisa May Alcott.
          p.   cm.
     Originally published: Boston: J. Redpath, 1863.
     "A BLS publication."
     ISBN 0-918222-78-8 : $7.95
     1. Alcott, Louisa May, 1832-1888.   2. United States—
History—Civil War, 1861-1865—Hospitals—Washington
(D.C.)   3. United States—History—Civil War, 1861-1865—
Personal narratives.   4. Washington (D.C.)—History—
Civil Way, 1861-1865—Hospitals.   5. Washington (D.C.)—
History—Civil War, 1861-1865—Personal narratives.
6. Nurses—Washington (D.C.)—Biography.   7. Authors,
American—Biography.   I. Title.
E621.A34   1993
973.7'76'092—dc20   92-47062
                                                      CIP

HOSPITAL SKETCHES.

CHAPTER I.

"I want something to do."

This remark being addressed to the world in general, no one in particular felt it their duty to reply ; so I repeated it to the smaller world about me, received the following suggestions, and settled the matter by answering my own inquiry, as people are apt to do when very much in earnest.

" Write a book," quoth the author of my being.

" Don't know enough, sir. First live, then write."

" Try teaching again," suggested my mother.

" No thank you, ma'am, ten years of that is enough."

" Take a husband like my Darby, and fulfill your mission," said sister Joan, home on a visit.

" Can't afford expensive luxuries, Mrs. Coobiddy."

" Turn actress, and immortalize your name," said sister Vashti, striking an attitude.

" I won't."

" Go nurse the soldiers," said my young neighbor, Tom, panting for " the tented field."

" I will !"

3

So far, very good. Here was the will, and plenty of it; now for the way. At first sight not a foot of it appeared; but that didn't matter, for the Periwinkles are a hopeful race. Their crest is an anchor, with three cock-a-doodles crowing atop. They all wear rose-colored spectacles, and are lineal descendants of the inventor of aerial architecture. An hour's conversation on the subject set the whole family in a blaze of enthusiasm. A model hospital was erected, and each member had accepted an honorable post therein. The paternal P. was chaplain, the maternal P. was matron, and all the youthful P.'s filled the pod of futurity with achievements whose brilliancy eclipsed the glories of the present and the past. Arriving at this satisfactory conclusion, the meeting adjourned; and the fact that Miss Tribulation was available as army nurse went abroad on the wings of the wind.

In a few days a townswoman heard of my desire, approved of it, and brought about an interview with one of the sisterhood which I wished to join, who was at home on a furlough, and able and willing to satisfy all inquiries. A morning chat with Miss General S.—we hear no end of Mrs. Generals, why not a Miss?—produced three results: I felt that I could do the work, was offered a place, and accepted it, promising not to desert, but stand ready to march on Washington at an hour's notice.

A few days were necessary for the letter containing my request and recommendation to reach headquarters, and another, containing my commission, to return; therefore no time was to be lost; and heartily thanking my pair of friends, I tore home through the December slush as if the rebels were after me, and like many another recruit, burst in upon my family with the announcement—

"I've enlisted!"

An impressive silence followed. Tom, the irrepressible, broke it with a slap on the shoulder and the graceful compliment—

" Old Trib, you're a trump !"

" Thank you ; then I'll *take* something :" which I did, in the shape of dinner, reeling off my news at the rate of three dozen words to a mouthful; and as every one else talked equally fast, and all together, the scene was most inspiring.

As boys going to sea immediately become nautical in speech, walk as if they already had their " sea legs " on, and shiver their timbers on all possible occasions, so I turned military at once, called my dinner my rations, saluted all new comers, and ordered a dress parade that very afternoon. Having reviewed every rag I possessed, I detailed some for picket duty while airing over the fence ; some to the sanitary influences of the wash-tub ; others to mount guard in the trunk ; while the weak and wounded went to the Work-basket Hospital, to be made ready for active service again. To this squad I devoted myself for a week ; but all was done, and I had time to get powerfully impatient before the letter came. It did arrive however, and brought a disappointment along with its good will and friendliness, for it told me that the place in the Armory Hospital that I supposed I was to take, was already filled, and a much less desirable one at Hurly-burly House was offered instead.

" That's just your luck, Trib. I'll take your trunk up garret for you again ; for of course you won't go," Tom remarked, with the disdainful pity which small boys affect when they get into their teens. I was wavering in my secret soul, but that settled the matter, and I crushed him on the spot with martial brevity—

" It is now one ; I shall march at six "

I have a confused recollection of spending the afternoon in pervading the house like an executive whirlwind, with my family swarming after me, all working, talking, prophesying and lamenting, while I packed my " go-abroady " possessions, tumbled the rest into two big boxes, danced on the lids till they shut, and gave them in charge, with the direction,—

" If I never come back, make a bonfire of them."

Then I choked down a cup of tea, generously salted instead of sugared, by some agitated relative, shouldered my knapsack—it was only a traveling bag, but do let me preserve the unities—hugged my family three times all round without a vestige of unmanly emotion, till a certain dear old lady broke down upon my neck, with a despairing sort of wail—

" Oh, my dear, my dear, how can I let you go ?"

" I'll stay if you say so, mother."

" But I don't ; go, and the Lord will take care of you."

Much of the Roman matron's courage had gone into the Yankee matron's composition, and, in spite of her tears, she would have sent ten sons to the war, had she possessed them, as freely as she sent one daughter, smiling and flapping on the door-step till I vanished, though the eyes that followed me were very dim, and the handkerchief she waved was very wet.

My transit from The Gables to the village depot was a funny mixture of good wishes and good byes, mud-puddles and shopping. A December twilight is not the most cheering time to enter upon a somewhat perilous enterprise, and, but for the presence of Vashti and neighbor Tom, I fear that I might have added a drop of the briny to the native moisture of—

" The town I left behind me ;"

though I'd no thought of giving out: oh, bless you, no ! When the engine screeched " Here we are," I clutched my escort in a fervent embrace, and skipped into the car with as blithe a farewell as if going on a bridal tour—though I believe brides don't usually wear cavernous black bonnets and fuzzy brown coats, with a hair-brush, a pair of rubbers, two books, and a bag of ginger-bread distorting the pockets of the same. If I thought that any one would believe it, I'd boldly state that I slept from C. to B., which would simplify matters immensely; but as I know they wouldn't, I'll confess that the head under the funereal coal-hod fermented with all manner of high thoughts and heroic purposes " to do or die,"— perhaps both; and the heart under the fuzzy brown coat felt very tender with the memory of the dear old lady, probably sobbing over her army socks and the loss of her topsy-turvy Trib. At this juncture I took the veil, and what I did behind it is nobody's business; but I maintain that the soldier who cries when his mother says " Good bye," is the boy to fight best, and die bravest, when the time comes, or go back to her better than he went.

Till nine o'clock I trotted about the city streets, doing those last errands which no woman would even go to heaven without attempting, if she could. Then I went to my usual refuge, and, fully intending to keep awake, as a sort of vigil appropriate to the occasion, fell fast asleep and dreamed propitious dreams till my rosy-faced cousin waked me with a kiss.

A bright day smiled upon my enterprise, and at ten I reported myself to my General, received last instructions and no end of the sympathetic encouragement which women give, in look, touch, and tone more effectually than in words. The next step was to get a free pass to Washington, for I'd no desire to waste my substance on railroad companies when " the boys " needed even a spinster's mite. A friend of mine had procured such a pass, and I was bent on doing likewise, though I had to face the president of the railroad to accomplish it   I'm a bashful individual, though I can't get any one to believe it; so it cost me a great effort to poke about the Worcester depot till the right door appeared, then walk into a room containing several gentlemen, and blunder out my request in a high state of stammer and blush. · Nothing could have been more courteous than this dreaded President, but it was evident that I had made as absurd a demand as if I had asked for the nose off his respectable face. He referred me to the Governor at the State House, and I backed out, leaving him no doubt to regret that such mild maniacs were left at large.   Here was a Scylla and Charybdis business : as if a President wasn't trying enough, without the Governor of Massachusetts and the Hub of the Hub on top of that.

" I never can do it," thought I.   " Tom will hoot at you if you don't," whispered the inconvenient little voice that is always goading people to the performance of disagreeable duties, and always appeals to the most effective agent to produce the proper result.   The idea of allowing any boy that ever wore a felt basin and a shoddy jacket with a microscopic tail, to crow over me, was preposterous, so giving myself a mental slap for such faint-heartedness, I streamed away across the Common, wondering if I ought to say " your Honor," or simply " Sir," and decided upon the latter, fortifying myself with recollections of an evening in a charming green library, where I beheld the Governor placidly consuming oysters, and laughing as if Massachusetts was a myth, and he had no heavier burden on his shoulders than his host's handsome hands.

Like an energetic fly in a very large cobweb, I struggled through the State House, getting into all the wrong rooms and none of the right, till I turned desperate, and went into one, resolving not to come out till I'd made somebody hear and answer me. I suspect that of all the wrong places I had blundered into, this was the most so. But I didn't care ; and, though the apartment was full of soldiers, surgeons, starers, and spittoons, I cornered a perfectly incapable person, and proceeded to pump for information with the following result :

" Was the Governor anywhere about ?"

No, he wasn't.

" Could he tell me where to look ?"

No, he couldn't.

" Did he know anything about free passes ?"

No, he didn't.

" Was there any one there of whom I could inquire ?"

Not a person.

" Did he know of any place where information could be obtained ?"

Not a place.

" Could he throw the smallest gleam of light upon the matter, in any way ?"

Not a ray.

I am naturally irascible, and if I could have shaken this negative gentleman vigorously, the relief would have been immense. The prejudices of society forbidding this mode of redress, I merely glowered at him ; and, before my wrath found vent in words, my General appeared, having seen me from an opposite window, and come to know what I was about. At her command the languid gentleman woke up, and troubled himself to remember that Major or Sergeant or something Mc K. knew all about the tickets, and his office was in Milk Street. I perked up instanter, and then, as if the exertion was too much for him, what did this animated wet blanket do but add—-

"I think Mc K. may have left Milk Street, now, and I don't know where he has gone."

"Never mind; the new comers will know where he has moved to, my dear, so don't be discouraged; and if you don't succeed, come to me, and we will see what to do next," said my General.

I blessed her in a fervent manner and a cool hall, fluttered round the corner, and bore down upon Milk street, bent on discovering Mc K. if such a being was to be found. He wasn't, and the ignorance of the neighborhood was really pitiable. Nobody knew anything, and after tumbling over bundles of leather, bumping against big boxes, being nearly annihilated by descending bales, and sworn at by aggravated truckmen, I finally elicited the advice to look for Mc K. in Haymarket Square. Who my informant was I've really forgotten; for, having hailed several busy gentlemen, some one of them fabricated this delusive quietus for the perturbed spirit, who instantly departed to the sequestered locality he named. If I had been in search of the Koh-i-noor diamond I should have been as likely to find it there as any vestige of Mc K. I stared at signs, inquired in shops, invaded an eating house, visited the recruiting tent in the middle of the Square, made myself a nuisance generally, and accumulated fine samples of mud from every gutter I fell into. All in vain; and I mournfully turned my face toward the General's, feeling that I should be forced to enrich the railroad company after all, when, suddenly, I beheld that admirable young man, brother-in-law Darby Coobiddy, Esq. I arrested him with a burst of news, and wants, and woes, which caused his manly countenance to lose its usual repose.

"Oh, my dear boy, I'm going to Washington at five, and I can't find the free ticket man, and there won't be time to see

Joan, and I'm so tired and cross I don't know what to do; and will you help me, like a cherub as you are?"

"Oh, yes, of course. I know a fellow who will set us right," responded Darby, mildly excited, and darting into some kind of an office, held counsel with an invisible angel, who sent him out radiant. "All serene. I've got him. I'll see you through the business, and then get Joan from the Dove Cote in time to see you off."

I'm a woman's rights woman, and if any man had offered help in the morning, I should have condescendingly refused it, sure that I could do everything as well, if not better, myself. My strong-mindedness had rather abated since then, and I was now quite ready to be a "timid trembler," if necessary. Dear me! how easily Darby did it all: he just asked one question, received an answer, tucked me under his arm, and in ten minutes I stood in the presence of Mc K., the Desired.

"Now my troubles are over," thought I, and as usual was direfully mistaken.

"You will have to get a pass from Dr. H., in Temple Place, before I can give you a pass, madam," answered Mc K., as blandly as if he wasn't carrying desolation to my soul. Oh, indeed! why didn't he send me to Dorchester Heights, India Wharf, or Bunker Hill Monument, and done with it? Here I was, after a morning's tramp, down in some place about Dock Square, and was told to step to Temple Place. Nor was that all; he might as well have asked me to catch a humming-bird, toast a salamander, or call on the man in the moon, as find a Doctor at home at the busiest hour of the day. It was a blow; but weariness had extinguished enthusiasm, and resignation clothed me as a garment. I sent Darby for Joan, and doggedly paddled off, feeling that mud was my native element, and quite sure that the evening papers would announce the appearance of the Wandering Jew, in feminine habili-ments.

"Is Dr. H. in ?"

"No, mum, he aint."

Of course he wasn't; I knew that before I asked: and, considering it all in the light of a hollow mockery, added:

"When will he probably return ?"

If the damsel had said, "ten to-night," I should have felt a grim satisfaction, in the fulfillment of my own dark prophecy; but she said, "At two, mum;" and I felt it a personal insult.

"I'll call, then. Tell him my business is important :" with which mysteriously delivered message I departed, hoping that I left her consumed with curiosity; for mud rendered me an object of interest.

By way of resting myself, I crossed the Common, for the third time, bespoke the carriage, got some lunch, packed my purchases, smoothed my plumage, and was back again, as the clock struck two. The Doctor hadn't come yet; and I was morally certain that he would not, till, having waited till the last minute, I was driven to buy a ticket, and, five minutes after the irrevocable deed was done, he would be at my serv-ice, with all manner of helpful documents and directions. Everything goes by contraries with me; so, having made up my mind to be disappointed, of course I wasn't; for, present-ly, in walked Dr. H., and no sooner had he heard my errand, and glanced at my credentials, than he said, with the most en gaging readiness:

"I will give you the order, with pleasure, madam."

Words connot express how soothing and delightful it was to find, at last, somebody who could do what I wanted, without sending me from Dan to Beersheba. for a dozen other bodies to do something else first. Peace descended, like oil, upon the ruffled waters of my being, as I sat listening to the busy scratch of his pen ; and, when he turned about, giving me not only the order, but a paper of directions wherewith to smooth away all difficulties between Boston and Washington, I felt as did poor Christian when the Evangelist gave him the scroll, on the safe side of the Slough of Despond. I've no doubt many dismal nurses have inflicted themselves upon the worthy gentleman since then ; but I am sure none have been more kindly helped, or are more grateful, than T. P. ; for that short interview added another to the many pleasant associations that already surround his name.

Feeling myself no longer a " Martha Struggles," but a comfortable young woman, with plain sailing before her, and the worst of the voyage well over, I once more presented myself to the valuable Mc K. The order was read, and certain printed papers, necessary to be filled out, were given a young gentleman—no, I prefer to say Boy, with a scornful emphasis upon the word, as the only means of revenge now left me. This Boy, instead of doing his duty with the diligence so charming in the young, loitered and lounged, in a manner which proved his education to have been sadly neglected in the—

" How doth the little busy bee,"

direction. He stared at me, gaped out of the window, ate peanuts, and gossiped with his neighbors—Boys, like himself, and all penned in a row, like colts at a Cattle Show. I don't imagine he knew the anguish he was inflicting ; for it was nearly three, the train left at five, and I had my ticket to get, my dinner to eat, my blessed sister to see, and the depot to reach, if I didn't die of apoplexy. Meanwhile Patience certainly had her perfect work that day, and I hope she enjoyed the job more than I did. Having waited some twenty minutes, it pleased this reprehensible Boy to make various marks and blots on my documents, toss them to a venerable creature of sixteen, who delivered them to me with such paternal directions, that it only needed a pat on the head and an encouraging—"Now run home to your Ma, little girl, and mind the crossings, my dear," to make the illusion quite perfect.

Why I was sent to a steamboat office for car tickets. is not for me to say, though I went as meekly as I should have gone to the Probate Court, if sent. A fat, easy gentleman gave me several bits of paper, with coupons attached, with a warning not to separate them, which instantly inspired me with a yearning to pluck them apart, and see what came of it. But, remembering through what fear and tribulation I had obtained them, I curbed Satan's promptings, and, clutching my prize, as if it were my pass to the Elysian Fields, I hurried home. Dinner was rapidly consumed; Joan enlightened, comforted, and kissed; the dearest of apple-faced cousins hugged; the kindest of apple-faced cousins' fathers subjected to the same process; and I mounted the ambulance, baggage-wagon, or anything you please but hack, and drove away, too tired to feel excited, sorry, or glad.

CHAPTER II.

A FORWARD MOVEMENT.

As travelers like to give their own impressions of a journey, though every inch of the road may have been described a half a dozen times before, I add some of the notes made by the way, hoping that they will amuse the reader, and convince the skeptical that such a being as Nurse Periwinkle does exist, that she really did go to Washington, and that these Sketches are not romance.

New York Train—Seven P. M.—Spinning along to take the boat at New London. Very comfortable ; munch gingerbread, and Mrs. C.'s fine pear, which deserves honorable mention, because my first loneliness was comforted by it, and pleasant recollections of both kindly sender and bearer. Look much at Dr. H.'s paper of directions—put my tickets in every conceivable place, that they may be get-at-able, and finish by losing them entirely. Suffer agonies till a compassionate neighbor pokes them out of a crack with his pen-knife. Put them in the inmost corner of my purse, that in the deepest recesses of my pocket, pile a collection of miscellaneous articles atop, and pin up the whole. Just get composed, feeling that I've done my best to keep them safely, when the Conductor appears, and I'm forced to rout them all out again, exposing my precautions, and getting into a flutter at keeping the man waiting. Finally, fasten them on the seat before me, and keep one eye steadily upon the yellow torments, till I forget all about them, in chat with the gentleman who shares my seat. Having heard complaints of the absurd way in which American women become images of petrified propriety, if addressed by strangers, when traveling alone, the inborn perversity of my nature causes me to assume an entirely opposite style of deportment; and, finding my companion hails from Little Athens, is acquainted with several of my three hundred and sixty-five cousins, and in every way a respectable and respectful member of society, I put my bashfulness in my pocket, and plunge into a long conversation on the war, the weather, music, Carlyle, skating, genius, hoops, and the immortality of the soul.

Ten, P. M.—Very sleepy. Nothing to be seen outside, but darkness made visible; nothing inside but every variety of bunch into which the human form can be twisted, rolled, or "massed," as Miss Prescott says of her jewels. Every man's legs sprawl drowsily, every woman's head (but mine,) nods, till it finally settles on somebody's shoulder, a new proof of the truth of the everlasting oak and vine simile; children fret; lovers whisper; old folks snore, and somebody privately imbibes brandy, when the lamps go out. The penetrating perfume rouses the multitude, causing some to start up, like war horses at the smell of powder. When the lamps are relighted, every one laughs, sniffs, and looks inquiringly at his neighbor—every one but a stout gentleman, who, with well-gloved hands folded upon his broad-cloth rotunuity, sleeps on impressively. Had he been innocent, he would have waked up ; for, to slumber in that babe-like manner, with a car full of giggling, staring, sniffing humanity, was simply preposterous. Public suspicion was down upon him at once. I doubt if the appearance of a flat black bottle with a label would have settled the matter more effectually than did the over dignified and profound repose of this short-sighted being. His moral neck-cloth, virtuous boots, and pious attitude availed him nothing, and it was well he kept his eyes shut, for " Humbug !" twinkled at him from every window-pane, brass nail and human eye around him.

Eleven, P. M.—In the boat "City of Boston," escorted thither by my car acquaintance, and deposited in the cabin. Trying to look as if the greater portion of my life had been passed on board boats, but painfully conscious that I don't know the first thing ; so sit bolt upright, and stare about me till I hear one lady say to another—"We must secure our berths at once ;" whereupon I dart at one, and, while leisurely taking off my cloak, wait to discover what the second move may be. Several ladies draw the curtains that hang in a semi-circle before each nest—instantly I whisk mine smartly together, and then peep out to see what next. Gradually, on hooks above the blue and yellow drapery, appear the coats and bonnets of my neighbors, while their boots and shoes, in every imaginable attitude, assert themselves below, as if their owners had committed suicide in a body. A violent creaking, scrambling, and fussing, causes the fact that people are going regularly to bed to dawn upon my mind. Of course they are ; and so am I—but pause at the seventh pin, remembering that, as I was born to be drowned, an eligible opportunity now presents itself ; and, having twice escaped a watery grave, the third immersion will certainly extinguish my vital spark. The boat is new, but if it ever intends to blow up, spring a leak, catch afire, or be run into, it will do the deed to-night, because I'm here to fulfill my destiny. With tragic calmness I resign myself, replace my pins, lash my purse and papers together, with my handkerchief, examine the saving circumference of my hoop, and look about me for any means of deliverance when the moist moment shall arrive ; for I've no intention of folding my hands and bubbling to death without an energetic splashing first. Barrels, hen-coops, portable settees, and life-preservers do not adorn the cabin, as they should ; and, roving wildly to and fro, my eye sees no ray of hope till it falls upon a plump old lady, devoutly reading in the cabin Bible, and a voluminous night-cap. I remember that, at the swimming school, fat girls always floated best, and in an instant my plan is laid. At the first alarm I firmly attach myself to the plump lady, and cling to her through fire and water ; for I feel that my old enemy, the cramp, will seize me by the foot, if I attempt to swim ; and, though I can hardly expect to reach Jersey City with myself and my baggage in as good condition as I hoped, I might manage to get picked up by holding to my fat friend ; if not it will be a comfort to feel that I've made an effort and shall die in good society. Poor dear woman ! how little she dreamed, as she read and rocked, with her cap in a high state of starch, and her feet comfortably cooking at the register, what fell designs were hovering about her, and how intently a small but determined eye watched her, till it suddenly closed.

Sleep got the better of fear to such an extent that my boots appeared to gape, and my bonnet nodded on its peg, before I gave in. Having piled my cloak, bag, rubbers, books and umbrella on the lower shelf, I drowsily swarmed on to the upper one, tumbling down a few times, and excoriating the knobby portions of my frame in the act. A very brief nap on the upper roost was enough to set me gasping as if a dozen feather beds and the whole boat were laid over me. Out I turned ; and, after a series of convulsions, which caused my neighbor to ask if I wanted the stewardess, I managed to get my luggage up and myself down. But even in the lower berth, my rest was not unbroken, for various articles kept dropping off the little shelf at the bottom of the bed, and every time I flew up, thinking my hour had come, I bumped my head severely against the little shelf at the top, evidently put there for that express purpose. At last, after listening to the swash of the waves outside, wondering if the machinery usually creaked in that way, and watching a knot-hole in the side of my berth, sure that death would creep in there as soon as I took my eye from it, I dropped asleep, and dreamed of muffins.

Five, A. M.—On deck, trying to wake up and enjoy an east wind and a morning fog, and a twilight sort of view of something on the shore. Rapidly achieve my purpose, and do enjoy every moment, as we go rushing through the Sound, with steamboats passing up and down, lights dancing on the shore, mist wreaths slowly furling off, and a pale pink sky above us, as the sun comes up.

Seven, A. M.—In the cars, at Jersey City. Much fuss with tickets, which one man scribbles over, another snips, and a third "makes note on." Partake of refreshment, in the gloom of a very large and dirty depot. Think that my sandwiches would be more relishing without so strong a flavor of napkin, and my gingerbread more easy of consumption if it had not been pulverized by being sat upon. People act as if early traveling didn't agree with them. Children scream and scamper ; men smoke and growl ; women shiver and fret ; porters swear; great truck horses pace up and down with loads of baggage; and every one seems to get into the wrong car, and come tumbling out again. One man, with three children, a dog, a bird-cage, and several bundles, puts himself and his possessions into every possible place where a man, three children, dog, bird-cage and bundles could be got, and is satisfied with none of them. I follow their movements, with an interest that is really exhausting, and, as they vanish, hope for rest, but don't get it. A strong-minded woman, with a tumbler in her hand, and no cloak or shawl on, comes rushing through the car, talking loudly to a small porter, who lugs a folding bed after her, and looks as if life were a burden to him.

"You promised to have it ready. It is not ready. It must be a car with a water jar, the windows must be shut, the fire must be kept up, the blinds must be down. No, this won't do. I shall go through the whole train, and suit myself, for you promised to have it ready. It is not ready," &c., all through again, like a hand-organ. She haunted the cars, the depot, the office and baggage-room, with her bed, her tumbler, and her tongue, till the train started; and a sense of fervent gratitude filled my soul, when I found that she and her unknown invalid were not to share our car.

Philadelphia.—An old place, full of Dutch women, in "bellus top" bonnets, selling vegetables, in long, open markets. Every one seems to be scrubbing their white steps. All the houses look like tidy jails, with their outside shutters. Several have crape on the door-handles, and many have flags flying from roof or balcony. Few men appear, and the women seem to do the business, which, perhaps, accounts for its being so well done. Pass fine buildings, but don't know what they are. Would like to stop and see my native city:

for, having left it at the tender age of two, my recollections are not vivid.

Baltimore.—A big, dirty, shippy, shiftless place, full of goats, geese, colored people, and coal, at least the part of it I see. Pass near the spot where the riot took place, and feel as if I should enjoy throwing a stone at somebody, hard. Find a guard at the ferry, the depot, and here and there, along the road. A camp whitens one hill-side, and a cavalry training school, or whatever it should be called, is a very interesting sight, with quantities of horses and riders galloping, marching, leaping, and skirmishing, over all manner of break-neck places. A party of English people get in—the men, with sandy hair and red whiskers, all trimmed alike, to a hair; rough grey coats, very rosy, clean faces, and a fine, full way of speaking, which is particularly agreeable, after our slipshod American gabble. The two ladies wear funny velvet fur-trimmed hoods; are done up, like compact bundles, in tartan shawls; and look as if bent on seeing everything thoroughly. The devotion of one elderly John Bull to his red-nosed spouse was really beautiful to behold. She was plain and cross, and fussy and stupid, but J. B., Esq., read no papers when she was awake, turned no cold shoulder when she wished to sleep, and cheerfully said, "Yes, me dear," to every wish or want the wife of his bosom expressed. I quite warmed to the excellent man, and asked a question or two, as the only means of expressing my good will. He answered very civilly, but evidently hadn't been used to being addressed by strange women in public conveyances; and Mrs. B. fixed her green eyes upon me, as if she thought me a forward huzzy, or whatever is good English for a presuming young woman. The pair left their friends before we reached Washington; and the last I saw of them was a vision of a large plaid lady, stalking

grimly away, on the arm of a rosy, stout gentleman, loaded
with rugs, bags, and books, but still devoted, still smiling, and
waving a hearty " Fare ye well !   We'll meet ye at Willard's
on Chusday."

Soon after their departure we had an accident ; for no long
journey in America would be complete without one.   A coup-
ling iron broke ; and, after leaving the last car behind us, we
waited for it to come up, which it did, with a crash that
knocked every one forward on their faces, and caused several
old ladies to screech dismally.   Hats flew off, bonnets were
flattened, the stove skip ed, the lamps fell down, the water
jar turned a somersault, and the wheel just over which I sat
received some damage.   Of course, it became necessary for
all the men to get out, and stand about in everybody's way,
while repairs were made ; and for the women to wrestle their
heads out of the windows, asking ninety-nine foolish questions
to one sensible one.   A few wise females seized this favorable
moment to better their seats, well knowing that few men can
face the wooden stare with which they regard the former pos-
sessors of the places they have invaded.

The country through which we passed did not seem so very
unlike that which I had left, except that it was more level and
less wintry.   In summer time the wide fields would have
shown me new sights, and the way-side hedges blossomed with
new flowers ; now, everything was sere and sodden, and a general air of shiftlessness prevailed, which would have caused a
New England farmer much disgust, and a strong desire to
" buckle to, " and " right up " things.   Dreary little houses,
with chimneys built outside, with clay and rough sticks piled
crosswise, as we used to build cob towers, stood in barren
looking fields, with cow, pig, or mule lounging about the door.
We often passed colored people, looking as if they had come

out of a picture book, or off the stage, but not at all the sort
of people I'd been accustomed to see at the North.

Way-side encampments made the fields and lanes gay with
blue coats and the glitter of buttons. Military washes flapped
and fluttered on the fences; pots were steaming in the open
air : all sorts of tableaux seen through the openings of tents,
and everywhere the boys threw up their caps and cut capers as
we passed.

Washington.—It was dark when we arrived ; and, but for
the presence of another friendly gentleman, I should have
yielded myself a helpless prey to the first overpowering hack-
man, who insisted that I wanted to go just where I didn't. Putting me into the conveyance I belonged in, my escort added
to the obligation by pointing out the objects of interest which
we passed in our long drive. Though I'd often been told that
Washington was a spacious place, its visible magnitude quite
took my breath away, and of course I quoted Randolph's
expression, " a city of magnificent distances," as I suppose
every one does when they see it. The Capitol was so like the
pictures that hang opposite the staring Father of his Country,
in boarding-houses and hotels, that it did not impress me,
except to recall the time when I was sure that Cinderella went
to housekeeping in just such a place, after she had married the
inflammable Prince ; though, even at that early period, I had
my doubts as to the wisdom of a match whose foundation was
of glass.

The White House was lighted up, and carriages were roll-
ing in and out of the great gate. I stared hard at the famous
East Room, and would have liked a peep through the crack of
the door. My old gentleman was indefatigable in his attentions, and I said " Splendid !" to everything he pointed out,
though I suspect I often admired the wrong place, and

missed the right.   Pennsylvania Avenue, with its bustle, lights, music, and military, made me feel as if I'd crossed the water and landed somewhere in Carnival time.   Coming to less noticeable parts of the city, my companion fell silent, and I meditated upon the perfection which Art had attained in America—having just passed a bronze statue of some hero, who looked like a black Methodist minister, in a cocked hat, above the waist, and a tipsy squire below ; while his horse stood like an opera dancer, on one leg, in a high, but somewhat re- markable wind, which blew his mane one way and his massive tail the other.

" Hurly-burly House, ma'am !" called a voice, startling me from my reverie, as we stopped before a great pile of build- ings, with a flag flying before it, sentinels at the door, and a very trying quantity of men lounging about.   My heart beat rather faster than usual, and it suddenly struck me that I was very far from home ; but I descended with dignity, wondering whether I should be stopped for want of a countersign, and forced to pass the night in the street.   Marching boldly up the steps, I found that no form was necessary, for the men fell back, the guard touched their caps, a boy opened the door, and, as it closed behind me, I felt that I was fairly started, and Nurse Periwinkle's Mission was begun.

begin to see hospital life in earnest, for you won't probably find time to sit down all day, and may think yourself fortunate if you get to bed by midnight. Come to me in the ball-room when you are ready; the worst cases are always carried there, and I shall need your help."

So saying, the energetic little woman twirled her hair into a button at the back of her head, in a " cleared for action " sort of style, and vanished, wrestling her way into a feminine kind of pea-jacket as she went.

I am free to confess that I had a realizing sense of the fact that my hospital bed was not a bed of roses just then, or the prospect before me one of unmingled rapture. My three days' experiences had begun with a death, and, owing to the defalcation of another nurse, a somewhat abrupt plunge into the superintendence of a ward containing forty beds, where I spent my shining hours washing faces, serving rations, giving medicine, and sitting in a very hard chair, with pneumonia on one side, diptheria on the other, two typhoids opposite, and a dozen dilapidated patriots, hopping, lying, and lounging about, all staring more or less at the new " nuss," who suffer-ed untold agonies, but concealed them under as matronly an aspect as a spinster could assume, and blundered through her trying labors with a Spartan firmness, which I hope they ap-preciated, but am afraid they didn't. Having a taste for " ghastliness," I had rather longed for the wounded to arrive, for rheumatism was n't heroic, neither was liver complaint, or measles ; even fever had lost its charms since " bathing burn-ing brows " had been used up in romances, real and ideal. But when I peeped into the dusky street lined with what I at first had innocently called market carts, now unloading their sad freight at our door, I recalled sundry reminiscences I had heard from nurses of longer standing, my ardor experienced a sudden chill, and I indulged in a most unpatriotic wish that I was safe at home again, with a quiet day before me, and no necessity for being hustled up, as if I were a hen and had only to hop off my roost, give my plumage a peck, and be ready for action. A second bang at the door sent this recreant desire to the right about, as a little woolly head popped in, and Joey, (a six years' old contraband,) announced—

"Miss Blank is jes' wild fer ye, and says fly round right away. They's comin' in, I tell yer, heaps on 'em—one was took out dead, and I see him,—hi! warn't he a goner!"

With which cheerful intelligence the imp scuttled away, singing like a blackbird, and I followed, feeling that Richard was *not* himself again, and wouldn't be for a long time to come.

The first thing I met was a regiment of the vilest odors that ever assaulted the human nose, and took it by storm. Cologne, with its seven and seventy evil savors, was a posy-bed to it; and the worst of this affliction was, every one had assured me that it was a chronic weakness of all hospitals, and I must bear it. I did, armed with lavender water, with which I so besprinkled myself and premises, that I was soon known among my patients as "the nurse with the bottle." Having been run over by three excited surgeons, bumped against by migratory coal-hods, water-pails, and small boys, nearly scalded by an avalanche of newly-filled tea-pots, and hopelessly entangled in a knot of colored sisters coming to wash, I progressed by slow stages up stairs and down, till the main hall was reached, and I paused to take breath and a survey. There they were! "our brave boys," as the papers justly call them, for cowards could hardly have been so riddled with shot and shell, so torn and shattered, nor have borne suffering for which we have no name.

with an uncomplaining fortitude, which made one glad to cherish each like a brother. In they came, some on stretchers, some in men's arms, some feebly staggering along propped on rude crutches, and one lay stark and still with covered face, as a comrade gave his name to be recorded before they carried him away to the dead house. All was hurry and confusion; the hall was full of these wrecks of humanity, for the most exhausted could not reach a bed till duly ticketed and registered; the walls were lined with rows of such as could sit, the floor covered with the more disabled, the steps and doorways filled with helpers and lookers on; the sound of many feet and voices made that usually quiet hour as noisy as noon; and, in the midst of it all, the matron's motherly face brought more comfort to many a poor soul, than the cordial draughts she administered, or the cheery words that welcomed all, making of the hospital a home.

The sight of several stretchers, each with its legless, armless, or desperately wounded occupant, entering my ward, admonished me that I was there to work, not to wonder or weep; so I corked up my feelings, and returned to the path of duty, which was rather " a hard road to travel " just then. The house had been a hotel before hospitals were needed, and many of the doors still bore their old names; some not so inappropriate as might be imagined, for that ward was in truth a *ball-room*, if gun-shot wounds could christen it. Forty beds were prepared, many already tenanted by tired men who fell down anywhere, and drowsed till the smell of food roused them. Round the great stove was gathered the dreariest group I ever saw—ragged, gaunt and pale, mud to the knees, with bloody bandages untouched since put on days before; many bundled up in blankets, coats being lost or useless; and all wearing that disheartened look which proclaimed defeat, more plainly than any telegram of the Burnside blunder. I pitied them so much, I dared not speak to them, though, remembering all they had been through since the fight at Fred. ericksburg, I yearned to serve the dreariest of them all.   Presently, Miss Blank tore me from my refuge behind piles of one-sleeved shirts, odd socks, bandages and lint ; put basin, sponge, towels, and a block of brown soap into my hands, with these appalling directions :

" Come, my dear, begin to wash as fast as you can. Tell them to take off socks, coats and shirts, scrub them well, put on clean shirts, and the attendants will finish them off, and lay them in bed."

If she had requested me to shave them all, or dance a hornpipe on the stove funnel, I should have been less staggered ; but to scrub some dozen lords of creation at a moment's notice, was really—really——. However, there was no time for nonsense. and, having resolved when I came to do everything I was bid, I drowned my scruples in my washbowl, clutched my soap manfully, and, assuming a business-like air, made a dab at the first dirty specimen I saw, bent on performing my task *vi et armis* if necessary. I chanced to light on a withered old Irishman, wounded in the head, which caused that portion of his frame to be tastefully laid out like a garden, the bandages being the walks, his hair the shrubbery. He was so overpowered by the honor of having a lady wash him, as he expressed it, that he did nothing but roll up his eyes, and bless me, in an irresistible style which was too much for my sense of the ludicrous ; so we laughed together, and when I knelt down to take off his shoes, he " flopped " also, and wouldn't hear of my touching " them dirty craters. May your bed above be aisy darlin', for the day's work ye are doon ! —Whoosh ! there ye are, and bedad, it's hard tellin' which is the dirtiest, the fut or the shoe." It was; and if he hadn't been to the fore, I should have gone on pulling, under the impression that the "fut" was a boot, for trousers, socks, shoes and legs were a mass of mud. This comical tableau produced a general grin, at which propitious beginning I took heart and scrubbed away like any tidy parent on a Saturday night. Some of them took the performance like sleepy children, leaning their tired heads against me as I worked, others looked grimly scandalized, and several of the roughest colored like bashful girls. One wore a soiled little bag about his neck, and, as I moved it, to bathe his wounded breast, I said,

"Your talisman didn't save you, did it?"

"Well, I reckon it did, marm, for that shot would a gone a couple a inches deeper but for my old mammy's camphor bag," answered the cheerful philosopher.

Another, with a gun-shot wound through the cheek, asked for a looking-glass, and when I brought one, regarded his swollen face with a dolorous expression, as he muttered—

"I vow to gosh, that's too bad! I warn't a bad looking chap before, and now I'm done for; won't there be a thunderin' scar? and what on earth will Josephine Skinner say?"

He looked up at me with his one eye so appealingly, that I controlled my risibles, and assured him that if Josephine was a girl of sense, she would admire the honorable scar, as a lasting proof that he had faced the enemy, for all women thought a wound the best decoration a brave soldier could wear. I hope Miss Skinner verified the good opinion I so rashly expressed of her, but I shall never know.

The next scrubbee was a nice-looking lad, with a curly brown mane, honest blue eyes, and a merry mouth. He lay on a bed, with one leg gone, and the right arm so shattered that it must evidently follow: yet the little sergeant was as merry as if his afflictions were not worth lamenting over; and when a drop or two of salt water mingled with my suds at the sight of this strong young body, so marred and maimed, the boy looked up, with a brave smile, though there was a little quiver of the lips, as he said,

"Now don't you fret yourself about me, miss; I'm first rate here, for it's nuts to lie still on this bed, after knocking about in those confounded ambulances, that shake what there is left of a fellow to jelly. I never was in one of these places before, and think this cleaning up a jolly thing for us, though I'm afraid it isn't for you ladies."

"Is this your first battle, Sergeant?"

"No, miss; I've been in six scrimmages, and never got a scratch till this last one; but it's done the business pretty thoroughly for me, I should say. Lord! what a scramble there'll be for arms and legs, when we old boys come out of our graves, on the Judgment Day: wonder if we shall get our own again? If we do, my leg will have to tramp from Fredericksburg, my arm from here, I suppose, and meet my body, wherever it may be."

The fancy seemed to tickle him mightily, for he laughed blithely, and so did I; which, no doubt, caused the new nurse to be regarded as a light-minded sinner by the Chaplain, who roamed vaguely about, with his hands in his pockets, preaching resignation to cold, hungry, wounded men, and evidently feeling himself, what he certainly was, the wrong man in the wrong place.

"I say, Mrs.!" called a voice behind me; and, turning, I saw a rough Michigander, with an arm blown off at the shoulder, and two or three bullets still in him — as he afterwards

mentioned, as carelessly as if gentlemen were in the habit of
carrying such trifles about with them. I went to him, and,
while administering a dose of soap and water, he whispered,
irefully :

"That red-headed devil, over yonder, is a reb, hang him !
He's got shet of a foot, or he'd a cut like the rest of the lot.
Don't you wash him, nor feed him, but jest let him holler till
he's tired. It's a blasted shame to fetch them fellers in here,
along side of us ; and so I'll tell the chap that bosses this
concern ; cuss me if I don't.

I regret to say that I did not deliver a moral sermon upon
the duty of forgiving our enemies, and the sin of profanity,
then and there ; but, being a red-hot Abolitionist, stared
fixedly at the tall rebel, who was a copperhead, in every sense
of the word, and privately resolved to put soap in his eyes,
rub his nose the wrong way, and excoriate his cuticle generally, if I had the washing of him.

My amiable intentions, however, were frustrated ; for, when
I approached. with as Christian an expression as my principles
would allow, and asked the question—"Shall I try to make
you more comfortable, sir ?" all I got for my pains was a
gruff—

"No ; I'll do it myself."

"Here's your Southern chivalry, with a witness," thought
I, dumping the basin down before him, thereby quenching a
strong desire to give him a summary baptism, in return for his
ungraciousness ; for my angry passions rose, at this rebuff, in
a way that would have scandalized good Dr. Watts. He was
a disappointment in all respects, (the rebel, not the blessed
Doctor,) for he was neither fiendish, romantic, pathetic, or
anything interesting ; but a long, fat man, with a head like a

burning bush, and a perfectly expressionless face : so I coul 1
dislike him without the slightest drawback, and ignored his
existence from that day forth. One redeeming trait he certainly
did possess, as the floor speedily testified ; for his ablutions
were so vigorously performed, that his bed soon stood like an
isolated island, in a sea of soap-suds, and he resembled a
dripping merman, suffering from the loss of a fin.   If clean-
liness is a near neighbor to godliness, then was the big rebel
the godliest man in my ward that day.

Having done up our human wash, and laid it out to dry, the
second syllable of our version of the word War-fare was enacted
with much success.   Great trays of bread, meat, soup and
coffee appeared ; and both nurses and attendants turned
waiters, serving bountiful rations to all who could eat.   I can
call my pinafore to testify to my good will in the work, for in
ten minutes it was reduced to a perambulating bill of fare, pre-
senting samples of all the refreshments going or gone.   It was
a lively scene ; the long room lined with rows of beds, each
filled by an occupant, whom water, shears, and clean raiment,
had transformed from a dismal ragamuffin into a recumbent
hero, with a cropped head.   To and fro rushed matrons, maids,
and convalescent " boys," skirmishing with knives and forks ;
retreating with empty plates ; marching and counter-marching,
with unvaried success, while the clash of busy spoons made
most inspiring music for the charge of our Light Brigade :

> " Beds to the front of them,
> Beds to the right of them,
> Beds to the left of them,
>   Nobody blundered.
> Beamed at by hungry souls,
> Screamed at with brimming bowls,
> Steamed at by army rolls,
>   Buttered and sundered.
> With coffee not cannon plied,
> Each must be satisfied,
> Whether they lived or died ;
>   All the men wondered."

Very welcome seemed the generous meal, after a week of suffering, exposure, and short commons; soon the brown faces began to smile, as food, warmth, and rest, did their pleasant work; and the grateful "Thankee's" were followed by more graphic accounts of the battle and retreat, than any paid reporter could have given us. Curious contrasts of the tragic and comic met one everywhere; and some touching as well as ludicrous episodes, might have been recorded that day. A six foot New Hampshire man, with a leg broken and perforated by a piece of shell, so large that, had I not seen the wound, I should have regarded the story as a Munchausenism, beckoned me to come and help him, as he could not sit up, and both his bed and beard were getting plentifully anointed with soup. As I fed my big nestling with corresponding mouthfuls, I asked him how he felt during the battle.

" Well, 'twas my fust, you see, so I aint ashamed to say I was a trifle flustered in the beginnin', there was such an allfired racket; for ef there's anything I do spleen agin, it's noise. But when my mate, Eph Sylvester, fell, with a bullet through his head, I got mad, and pitched in, licketty cut. Our part of the fight didn't last long; so a lot of us larked round Fredericksburg, and give some of them houses a pretty consid'able of a rummage, till we was ordered out of the mess. Some of our fellows cut like time; but I warn't a-goin to run for nobody; and, fust thing I knew, a shell bust, right in front of us, and I keeled over, feelin' as if I was blowed higher'n a kite. I sung out, and the boys come back for me, double quick; but the way they chucked me over them fences was a caution, I tell you. Next day I was most as black as that darkey yonder, lickin' plates on the sly. This is bully coffee, ain't it? Give us another pull at it, and I'll be obleeged to you."

I did ; and, as the last gulp subsided, he said, with a rub
of his old handkerchief over eyes as well as mouth :

" Look a here; I've got a pair a earbobs and a handkercher
pin I'm a goin' to give you, if you'll have them ; for you're
the very moral o' Lizy Sylvester, poor Eph's wife : that's why
I signalled you to come over here.   They aint much, I guess,
but they'll do to memorize the rebs by."

Burrowing under his pillow, he produced a little bundle of
what he called " truck," and gallantly presented me with a
pair of earrings, each representing a cluster of corpulent
grapes, and the pin a basket of astonishing fruit, the whole
large and coppery enough for a small warming-pan.   Feeling
delicate about depriving him of such valuable relics, I accepted
the earrings alone, and was obliged to depart, somewhat
abruptly, when my friend stuck the warming-pan in the bosom
of his night-gown, viewing it with much complacency, and,
perhaps, some tender memory, in that rough heart of his, for
the comrade he had lost.

Observing that the man next him had left his meal untouched,
I offered the same service I had performed for his neighbor,
but he shook his head.

" Thank you, ma'am ; I don't think I'll ever eat again, for
I'm shot in the stomach.   But I'd like a drink of water, if
you aint too busy."

I rushed away, but the water-pails were gone to be refilled,
and it was some time before they reappeared.   I did not forget my patient patient, meanwhile, and, with the first mugful,
hurried back to him.   He seemed asleep ; but something in
the tired white face caused me to listen at his lips for a breath.
None came.   I touched his forehead ; it was cold : and then I
knew that, while he waited, a better nurse than I had given
him a cooler draught, and healed him with a touch.   I laid

the sheet over the quiet sleeper, whom no noise could now
disturb; and, half an hour later, the bed was empty. It
seemed a poor requital for all he had sacrificed and suffered,
—that hospital bed, lonely even in a crowd; for there was no
familiar face for him to look his last upon; no friendly voice
to say, Good bye; no hand to lead him gently down into the
Valley of the Shadow; and he vanished, like a drop in that
red sea upon whose shores so many women stand lamenting.
For a moment I felt bitterly indignant at this seeming care-
lessness of the value of life, the sanctity of death; then consoled myself with the thought that, when the great muster
roll was called, these nameless men might be promoted above
many whose tall monuments record the barren honors they
have won.

All having eaten, drank, and rested, the surgeons began
their rounds; and I took my first lesson in the art of dressing
wounds. It wasn't a festive scene, by any means; for Dr
P., whose Aid I constituted myself, fell to work with a vigor
which soon convinced me that I was a weaker vessel, though
nothing would have induced me to confess it then. He had
served in the Crimea, and seemed to regard a dilapidated body
very much as I should have regarded a damaged garment;
and, turning up his cuffs, whipped out a very unpleasant looking housewife, cutting, sawing, patching and piecing, with the
enthusiasm of an accomplished surgical seamstress; explaining
the process, in scientific terms, to the patient, meantime;
which, of course, was immensely cheering and comfortable.
There was an uncanny sort of fascination in watching him, as
he peered and probed into the mechanism of those wonderful
bodies, whose mysteries he understood so well. The more
intricate the wound, the better he liked it. A poor private,
with both legs off, and shot through the lungs, possessed more

attractions for him than a dozen generals, slightly scratched in some " masterly retreat ;" and had any one appeared in small pieces, requesting to be put together again, he would have considered it a special dispensation.

The amputations were reserved till the morrow, and the merciful magic of ether was not thought necessary that day, so the poor souls had to bear their pains as best they might. It is all very well to talk of the patience of woman ; and far be it from me to pluck that feather from her cap, for, heaven knows, she isn't allowed to wear many; but the patient endurance of these men, under trials of the flesh, was truly wonderful. Their fortitude seemed contagious, and scarcely a cry escaped them, though I often longed to groan for them, when pride kept their white lips shut, while great drops stood upon their foreheads, and the bed shook with the irrepressible tremor of their tortured bodies. One or two Irishmen anathematized the doctors with the frankness of their nation, and ordered the Virgin to stand by them, as if she had been the wedded Biddy to whom they could administer the poker, if she didn't ; but, as a general thing, the work went on in silence, broken only by some quiet request for roller, instruments, or plaster, a sigh from the patient, or a sympathizing murmur from the nurse.

It was long past noon before these repairs were even partially made ; and, having got the bodies of my boys into something like order, the next task was to minister to their minds, by writing letters to the anxious souls at home ; answering questions, reading papers, taking possession of money and valuables ; for the eighth commandmnnt was reduced to a very fragmentary condition, both by the blacks and whites, who ornamented our hospital with their presence. Pocket books, purses, miniatures, and watches, were sealed up, labelled, and handed over to the matron, till such times as the owners thereof were ready to depart homeward or campward again.   The letters dictated to me, and revised by me, that afternoon, would have made an excellent chapter for some future history of the war; for, like that which Thackeray's " Ensign Spooney " wrote his mother just before Waterloo, they were " full of affection, pluck, and bad spelling ;" nearly all giving lively accounts of the battle, and ending with a somewhat sudden plunge from patriotism to provender , desiring " Marm," " Mary Ann," or " Aunt Peters," to send along some pies, pickles, sweet stuff, and apples, " to yourn in haste," Joe, Sam, or Ned, as the case might be.

My little Sergeant insisted on trying to scribble something with his left hand, and patiently accomplished some half dozen lines of hieroglyphics, which he gave me to fold and direct, with a boyish blush, that rendered a glimpse of " My Dearest Jane," unnecessary, to assure me that the heroic lad had been more successful in the service of Commander-in-Chief Cupid than that of Gen. Mars ; and a charming little romance blossomed instanter in Nurse Periwinkle's romantic fancy, though no further confidences were made that day, for Sergeant fell asleep, and, judging from his tranquil face, visited his absent sweetheart in the pleasant land of dreams.

At five o'clock a great bell rang, and the attendants flew, not to arms, but to their trays, to bring up supper, when a second uproar announced that it was ready.   The new comers woke at the sound ; and I presently discovered that it took a very bad wound to incapacitate the defenders of the faith for the consumption of their rations ; the amount that some of them sequestered was amazing ; but when I suggested the probability of a famine hereafter, to the matron, that motherly lady cried out : " Bless their hearts, why shouldn't they eat ?

It's their only amusement; so fill every one, and, if there's not enough ready to-night, I'll lend my share to the Lord by giving it to the boys." And, whipping up her coffee-pot and plate of toast, she gladdened the eyes and stomachs of two or three dissatisfied heroes, by serving them with a liberal hand; and I haven't the slightest doubt that, having cast her bread upon the waters, it came back buttered, as another large-hearted old lady was wont to say.

Then came the doctor's evening visit; the administration of medicines; washing feverish faces; smoothing tumbled beds; wetting wounds; singing lullabies; and preparations for the night. By twelve, the last labor of love was done; the last " good night " spoken; and, if any needed a reward for that day's work, they surely received it, in the silent eloquence of those long lines of faces, showing pale and peaceful in the shaded rooms, as we quitted them, followed by grateful glances that lighted us to bed, where rest, the sweetest, made our pillows soft, while Night and Nature took our places, filling that great house of pain with the healing miracles of Sleep, and his diviner brother, Death.

CHAPTER IV.

A NIGHT

Being fond of the night side of nature, I was soon promoted to the post of night nurse, with every facility for indulging in my favorite pastime of "owling." My colleague, a black eyed widow, relieved me at dawn, we two taking care of the ward between us, like regular nurses, turn and turn about. I usually found my boys in the jolliest state of mind their condition allowed; for it was a known fact that Nurse Periwinkle objected to blue devils, and entertained a belief that he who laughed most was surest of recovery. At the beginning of my reign, dumps and dismals prevailed; the nurses looked anxious and tired, the men gloomy or sad; and a general "Hark!-from-the-tombs-a-doleful-sound" style of conversation seemed to be the fashion: a state of things which caused one coming from a merry, social New England town, to feel as if she had got into an exhausted receiver; and the instinct of self-preservation, to say nothing of a philanthropic desire to serve the race, caused a speedy change in Ward No. 1.

More flattering than the most gracefully turned compliment, more grateful than the most admiring glance, was the sight of those rows of faces, all strange to me a little while ago, now lighting up, with smiles of welcome, as I came among them, enjoying that moment heartily, with a womanly pride in their regard, a motherly affection for them all. The evenings were spent in reading aloud, writing letters, waiting on and amusing the men, going the rounds with Dr. P., as he made his second daily survey, dressing my dozen wounds afresh, giving last doses, and making them cozy for the long hours to come, till the nine o'clock bell rang, the gas was turned down, the day nurses went off duty, the night watch came on, and my nocturnal adventures began.

My ward was now divided into three rooms; and, under favor of the matron, I had managed to sort out the patients in such a way that I had what I called, "my duty room," my "pleasure room," and my "pathetic room," and worked for each in a different way. One, I visited, armed with a dressing tray, full of rollers, plasters, and pins; another, with books, flowers, games, and gossip; a third, with teapots, lullabies, consolation, and, sometimes, a shroud.

Wherever the sickest or most helpless man chanced to be, there I held my watch, often visiting the other rooms, to see that the general watchman of the ward did his duty by the fires and the wounds, the latter needing constant wetting. Not only on this account did I meander, but also to get fresher air than the close rooms afforded; for, owing to the stupidity of that mysterious "somebody" who does all the damage in the world, the windows had been carefully nailed down above, and the lower sashes could only be raised in the mildest weather, for the men lay just below. I had suggested a summary smashing of a few panes here and there, when frequent appeals to headquarters had proved unavailing, and daily orders to lazy attendants had come to nothing. No one seconded the motion, however, and the nails were far beyond my reach ; for, though belonging to the sisterhood of " ministering angels," I had no wings, and might as well have asked for a suspension bridge, as a pair of steps, in that charitable chaos.

One of the harmless ghosts who bore me company during the haunted hours, was Dan, the watchman, whom I regarded with a certain awe ; for, though so much together, I never fairly saw his face, and, but for his legs, should never have recognized him, as we seldom met by day. These legs were remarkable, as was his whole figure, for his body was short, rotund, and done up in a big jacket, and muffler ; his beard hid the lower part of his face, his hat-brim the upper ; and all I ever discovered was a pair of sleepy eyes, and a very mild voice. But the legs ! — very long, very thin, very crooked and feeble, looking like gray sausages in their tight coverings, and finished off with a pair of expansive, green cloth shoes, very like Chinese junks with the sails down. This figure, gliding noiselessly about the dimly-lighted rooms, was strongly suggestive of the spirit of a beer-barrel mounted on cork-screws, haunting the old hotel in search of its lost mates, emptied and staved in long ago.

Another goblin who frequently appeared to me, was the attendant of "the pathetic room," who, being a faithful soul, was often up to tend two or three men, weak and wandering as babies, after the fever had gone. The amiable creature beguiled the watches of the night by brewing jorums of a fearful beverage, which he called coffee, and insisted on sharing with me ; coming in with a great bowl of something like mud soup, scalding hot, guiltless of cream, rich in an all-pervading flavor of molasses, scorch and tin pot. Such an amount of good will and neighborly kindness also went into the mess, that I never could find the heart to refuse, but always received it with thanks, sipped it with hypocritical relish while he remained, and whipped it into the slop-jar the instant he departed, thereby gratifying him, securing one rousing laugh in the doziest hour of the night, and no one was the worse for the transaction but the pigs. Whether they were " cut off untimely in their sins," or not, I carefully abstained from inquiring.

It was a strange life — asleep half the day, exploring Washington the other half, and all night hovering, like a massive cherubim, in a red rigolette, over the slumbering sons i.f man. I liked it, and found many things to amuse, instruct, and interest me. The snores alone were quite a study, varying from the mild sniff to the stentorian snort, which startled the echoes and hoisted the performer erect to accuse his neighbor of the deed, magnanimously forgive him, and, wrapping the drapery of his couch about him, lie down to vocal slumber. After listening for a week to this band of wind instruments, I indulged in the belief that I could recognize each by the snore alone, and was tempted to join the chorus by breaking out with John Brown's favorite hymn :

" Blow ye the trumpet, blow!"

I would have given much to have possessed the art of sketching, for many of the faces became wonderfully interesting when unconscious. Some grew stern and grim, the men evidently dreaming of war, as they gave orders, groaned over their wounds, or damned the rebels vigorously ; some grew sad and infinitely pathetic, as if the pain borne silently all day, re. venged itself by now betraying what the man's pride had concealed so well. Often the roughest grew young and pleasant

when sleep smoothed the hard lines away, letting the real nature
assert itself; many almost seemed to speak, and I learned to
know these men better by night than through any intercourse
by day. Sometimes they disappointed me, for faces that looked
merry and good in the light, grew bad and sly when the shad-
ows came; and though they made no confidences in words, I
read their lives, leaving them to wonder at the change of manner this midnight magic wrought in their nurse. A few talked
busily; one drummer boy sang sweetly, though no persuasions
could win a note from him by day; and several depended on
being told what they had talked of in the morning. Even my
constitutionals in the chilly halls, possessed a certain charm,
for the house was never still. Sentinels tramped round it all
night long, their muskets glittering in the wintry moonlight as
they walked, or stood before the doors, straight and silent, as
figures of stone, causing one to conjure up romantic visions of
guarded forts, sudden surprises, and daring deeds; for in
these war times the hum drum life of Yankeedom has vanished,
and the most prosaic feel some thrill of that excitement which
stirs the nation's heart, and makes its capital a camp of hospitals. Wandering up and down these lower halls, I often heard
cries from above, steps hurrying to and fro, saw surgeons
passing up, or men coming down carrying a stretcher, where
lay a long white figure, whose face was shrouded and whose
fight was done. Sometimes I stopped to watch the passers in
the street, the moonlight shining on the spire opposite, or the
gleam of some vessel floating, like a white-winged sea-gull,
down the broad Potomac, whose fullest flow can never wash
away the red stain of the land.

The night whose events I have a fancy to record, opened
with a little comedy, and closed with a great tragedy; for a
virtuous and useful life untimely ended is always tragical to

those who see not as God sees. My headquarters were beside
the bed of a New Jersey boy, crazed by the horrors of that
dreadful Saturday. A slight wound in the knee brought him
there ; but his mind had suffered more than his body ; some
string of that delicate machine was over strained, and, for
days, he had been re-living in imagination, the scenes he could
not forget, till his distress broke out in incoherent ravings,
pitiful to hear. As I sat by him, endeavoring to soothe his
poor distracted brain by the constant touch of wet hands over
his hot forehead, he lay cheering his comrades on, hurrying
them back, then counting them as they fell around him, often
clutching my arm, to drag me from the vicinity of a bursting
shell, or covering up his head to screen himself from a shower
of shot ; his face brilliant with fever ; his eyes restless ; his
head never still ; every muscle strained and rigid ; while an
incessant stream of defiant shouts, whispered warnings, and
broken laments, poured from his lips with that forceful bewil-
derment which makes such wanderings so hard to overhear.

It was past eleven, and my patient was slowly wearying
himself into fitful intervals of quietude, when, in one of these
pauses, a curious sound arrested my attention. Looking over
my shoulder, I saw a one-legged phantom hopping nimbly
down the room ; and, going to meet it, recognized a certain
Pennsylvania gentleman, whose wound-fever had taken a turn
for the worse, and, depriving him of the few wits a drunken
campaign had left him, set him literally tripping on the light,
fantastic toe " toward home," as he blandly informed me,
touching the military cap which formed a striking contrast to
the severe simplicity of the rest of his *undress* uniform.
When sane, the least movement produced a roar of pain or
a volley of oaths ; but the departure of reason seemed to
have wrought an agreeable change, both in the man and his

laugh together, my Prussian ally and myself were returning to our places, when the echo of a sob caused us to glance along the beds. It came from one in the corner — such a little bed! — and such a tearful little face looked up at us, as we stopped beside it! The twelve years old drummer boy was not sing-ing now, but sobbing, with a manly effort all the while to stifle the distressful sounds that would break out.

"What is it, Billy?" I asked, as he rubbed the tears away, and checked himself in the middle of a great sob to answer plaintively:

"I've got a chill, ma'am, but I aint cryin' for that, 'cause I'm used to it. I dreamed Kit was here, and when I waked up he wasn't, and I couldn't help it, then."

The boy came in with the rest, and the man who was taken dead from the ambulance was the Kit he mourned. Well he might; for, when the wounded were brought from Fredericks-burg, the child lay in one of the camps thereabout, and this good friend, though sorely hurt himself, would not leave him to the exposure and neglect of such a time and place; but, wrapping him in his own blanket, carried him in his arms to the transport, tended him during the passage, and only yielded up his charge when Death met him at the door of the hospital which promised care and comfort for the boy. For ten days, Billy had burned or shivered with fever and ague, pining the while for Kit, and refusing to be comforted, because he had not been able to thank him for the generous protection, which, perhaps, had cost the giver's life. The vivid dream had wrung the childish heart with a fresh pang, and when I tried the solace fitted for his years, the remorseful fear that haunted him found vent in a fresh burst of tears, as he looked at the wasted hands I was endeavoring to warm:

Oh! if I'd only been as thin when Kit carried me as I am

now, maybe he wouldn't have died; but I was heavy, he was
hurt worser than we knew, and so it killed him; and I didn't
see him, to say good bye."

This thought had troubled him in secret; and my assur-
ances that his friend would probably have died at all events,
hardly assuaged the bitterness of his regretful grief.

At this juncture, the delirious man began to shout; the one-
legged rose up in his bed, as if preparing for another dart,
Billy bewailed himself more piteously than before: and if
ever a woman was at her wit's end, that distracted female was
Nurse Periwinkle, during the space of two or three minutes,
as she vibrated between the three beds, like an agitated pen-
dulum. Like a most opportune reinforcement, Dan, the bandy,
appeared, and devoted himself to the lively party, leaving me
free to return to my post; for the Prussian, with a nod and a
smile, took the lad away to his own bed, and lulled him to
sleep with a soothing murmur, like a mammoth humble bee
I liked that in Fritz, and if he ever wondered afterward at the
dainties which sometimes found their way into his rations, or
the extra comforts of his bed, he might have found a solution
of the mystery in sundry persons' knowledge of the fatherly
action of that night.

Hardly was I settled again, when the inevitable bowl
appeared, and its bearer delivered a message I had expected,
yet dreaded to receive :

"John is going, ma'am, and wants to see you, if you can
come."

"The moment this boy is asleep; tell him so, and let me
know if I am in danger of being too late."

My, Ganymede departed, and while I quieted poor Shaw, I
thought of John. He came in a day or two after the others;
and, one evening, when I entered my "pathetic room," I

found a lately emptied bed occupied by a large, fair man, with a fine face, and the serenest eyes I ever met. One of the earlier comers had often spoken of a friend, who had remained behind, that those apparently worse wounded than himself might reach a shelter first. It seemed a David and Jonathan sort of friendship. The man fretted for his mate, and was never tired of praising John—his courage, sobriety, self-denial, and unfailing kindliness of heart; always winding up with: " He's an out an' out fine feller, ma'am; you see if he aint."

I had some curiosity to behold this piece of excellence, and when he came, watched him for a night or two, before I made friends with him ; for, to tell the truth, I was a little afraid of the stately looking man, whose bed had to be lengthened to accommodate his commanding stature ; who seldom spoke, uttered no complaint, asked no sympathy, but tranquilly observed what went on about him ; and, as he lay high upon his pillows, no picture of dying statesman or warrior was ever fuller of real dignity than this Virginia blacksmith. A most attractive face he had, framed in brown hair and beard, comely featured and full of vigor, as yet unsubdued by pain ; thought-ful and often beautifully mild while watching the afflictions of others, as if entirely forgetful of his own. His mouth was grave and firm, with plenty of will and courage in its lines, but a smile could make it as sweet as any woman's ; and his eyes were child's eyes, looking one fairly in the face, with a clear, straightforward glance, which promised well for such as placed their faith in him. He seemed to cling to life, as if it were rich in duties and delights, and he had learned the secret of content. The only time I saw his composure disturbed, was when my surgeon brought another to examine John, who scrutinized their faces with an anxious look, asking of the elder : " Do you think I shall pull through, sir ?" " I hope so, my man." And, as the two passed on. John's eye still followed them, with an intentness which would have won a truer answer from them, had they seen it. A momentary shadow flitted over his face ; then came the usual serenity, as if, in that brief eclipse, he had acknowledged the existence of some hard possibility, and, asking nothing yet hoping all things, left the issue in God's hands, with that submission which is true piety.

The next night, as I went my rounds with Dr. P., I happened to ask which man in the room probably suffered most ; and, to my great surprise, he glanced at John :

" Every breath he draws is like a stab ; for the ball pierced the left lung, broke a rib, and did no end of damage here and there ; so the poor lad can find neither forgetfulness nor ease, because he must lie on his wounded back or suffocate. It will be a hard struggle, and a long one, for he possesses great vitality ; but even his temperate life can't save him ; I wish it could."

" You don't mean he must die, Doctor ?"

" Bless you, there's not the slightest hope for him ; and you'd better tell him so before long ; women have a way of doing such things comfortably, so I leave it to you. He won't last more than a day or two, at furthest."

I could have sat down on the spot and cried heartily, if I had not learned the wisdom of bottling up one's tears for leisure moments. Such an end seemed very hard for such a man, when half a dozen worn out, worthless bodies round him, were gathering up the remnants of wasted lives, to linger on for years perhaps, burdens to others, daily reproaches to themselves. The army needed men like John, earnest, brave, and faithful ; fighting for liberty and justice with both heart and hand, true soldiers of the Lord. I could not give him up so soon, or think with any patience of so excellent a nature robbed of its fulfiment, and blundered into eternity by the rashness or stupidity of those at whose hands so many lives may be required. It was an easy thing for Dr. P. to say: "Tell him he must die," but a cruelly hard thing to do, and oy no means as "comfortable" as he politely suggested. I had not the heart to do it then, and privately indulged the hope that some change for the better might take place, in spite of gloomy prophesies; so, rendering my task unnecessary.

A few minutes later, as I came in again, with fresh rollers, I saw John sitting erect, with no one to support him, while the surgeon dressed his back. I had never hitherto seen it done; for, having simpler wounds to attend to, and knowing the fidelity of the attendant, I had left John to him, thinking it might be more agreeable and safe; for both strength and experience were needed in his case. I had forgotten that the strong man might long for the gentle tendance of a woman's hands, the sympathetic magnetism of a woman's presence, as well as the feebler souls about him. The Doctor's words caused me to reproach myself with neglect, not of any real duty perhaps, but of those little cares and kindnesses that solace homesick spirits, and make the heavy hours pass easier. John looked lonely and forsaken just then, as he sat with bent head, hands folded on his knee, and no outward sign of suffering, till, looking nearer, I saw great tears roll down and drop upon the floor. It was a new sight there; for, though I had seen many suffer, some swore, some groaned, most endured silently, but none wept. Yet it did not seem weak, only very touching, and straightway my fear vanished, my heart opened wide and took him in, as, gathering the bent head in my arms, as freely as if he had been a little child, I said, "Let me help you bear it, John."

Never, on any human countenance, have I seen so swift and beautiful a look of gratitude, surprise and comfort, as that which answered me more eloquently than the whispered—

"Thank you, ma'am, this is right good! this is what I wanted!"

"Then why not ask for it before?"

"I didn't like to be a trouble; you seemed so busy, and I could manage to get on alone."

"You shall not want it any more, John."

Nor did he; for now I understood the wistful look that sometimes followed me, as I went out, after a brief pause beside his bed, or merely a passing nod, while busied with those who seemed to need me more than he, because more urgent in their demands. Now I knew that to him, as to so many, I was the poor substitute for mother, wife, or sister. and in his eyes no stranger, but a friend who hitherto had seemed neglectful; for, in his modesty, he had never guessed the truth. This was changed now; and, through the tedious operation of probing, bathing, and dressing his wounds, he leaned against me, holding my hand fast, and, if pain wrung further tears from him, no one saw them fall but me. When he was laid down again, I hovered about him, in a remorseful state of mind that would not let me rest, till I had bathed his face, brushed his bonny brown hair, set all things smooth about him, and laid a knot of heath and heliotrope on his clean pillow. While doing this, he watched me with the satisfied expression I so liked to see; and when I offered the little nosegay, held it carefully in his great hand, smoothed a ruffled leaf or two, surveyed and smelt it with an air of genuine delight, and lay contentedly regarding the glimmer of the sunshine on the green. Although the manliest man among my forty, he said, " Yes, ma'am," like a little boy; received suggestions for his comfort with the quick smile that brightened his whole face; and now and then, as I stood tidying the table by his bed, I felt him softly touch my gown, as if to assure himself that I was there. Anything more natural and frank I never saw, and found this brave John as bashful as brave, yet full of excellencies and fine aspirations, which, having no power to express themselves in words, seemed to have bloomed into his character and made him what he was.

After that night, an hour of each evening that remained to him was devoted to his ease or pleasure. He could not talk much, for breath was precious, and he spoke in whispers; but from occasional conversations, I gleaned scraps of private history which only added to the affection and respect I felt for him. Once he asked me to write a letter, and as I settled pen and paper, I said, with an irrepressible glimmer of feminine curiosity, " Shall it be addressed to wife, or mother, John ?"

" Neither, ma'am; I've got no wife, and will write to mother myself when I get better. Did you think I was married because of this ?" he asked, touching a plain ring he wore, and often turned thoughtfully on his finger when he lay alone.

" Partly that, but more from a settled sort of look you have; a look which young men seldom get until they marry."

" I didn't know that; but I'm not so very young, ma'am, thirty in May, and have been what you might call settled this ten years. Mother's a widow, I'm the oldest child she has, and it wouldn't do for me to marry until Lizzy has a home of her own, and Jack's learned his trade; for we're not rich, and I must be father to the children and husband to the dear old woman, if I can."

" No doubt but you are both, John ; yet how came you to go to war, if you felt so ? Wasn't enlisting as bad as marrying ?"

" No, ma'am, not as I see it, for one is helping my neighbor, the other pleasing myself. I went because I couldn't help it. I didn't want the glory or the pay ; I wanted the right thing done, and people kept saying the men who were in earnest ought to fight. I was in earnest, the Lord knows ! but I held off as long as I could, not knowing which was my duty. Mother saw the case, gave me her ring to keep me steady, and said ' Go :' so I went."

A short story and a simple one, but the man and the mother were portrayed better than pages of fine writing could have done it.

" Do you ever regret that you came, when you lie here suffering so much ?"

" Never, ma'am ; I haven't helped a great deal, but I've shown I was willing to give my life, and perhaps I've got to ; but I don't blame anybody, and if it was to do over again, I'd do it. I'm a little sorry I wasn't wounded in front ; it looks cowardly to be hit in the back, but I obeyed orders, and it don't matter in the end, I know."

Poor John ! it did not matter now, except that a shot in front might have spared the long agony in store for him. He seemed to read the thought that troubled me, as he spoke so hopefully when there was no hope, for he suddenly added :

" This is my first battle ; do they think it's going to be my last ?"

" I'm afraid they do, John."

It was the hardest question I had ever been called upon to answer ; doubly hard with those clear eyes fixed on mine, forcing a truthful answer by their own truth He seemed a little startled at first, pondered over the fateful fact a moment, then shook his head, with a glance at the broad chest and muscular limbs stretched out before him :

" I'm not afraid, but it's difficult to believe all at once. I'm so strong it don't seem possible for such a little wound to kill me."

Merry Mercutio's dying words glanced through my memory as he spoke : " 'Tis not so deep as a well, nor so wide as a church door, but 'tis enough." And John would have said the same could he have seen the ominous black holes between his shoulders ; he never had, but, seeing the ghastly sights about him, could not believe his own wound more fatal than these, for all the suffering it caused him.

" Shall I write to your mother, now ?" I asked, thinking that these sudden tidings might change all plans and puposes. But they did not ; for the man received the order of the Divine Commander to march with the same unquestioning obedience with which the soldier had received that of the human one ; doubtless remembering that the first led him to life, and the last to death.

" No, ma'am ; to Jack just the same ; he'll break it to her best, and I'll add a line to her myself when you get done."

So I wrote the letter which he dictated, finding it better than any I had sent ; for, though here and there a little ungrammatical or inelegant, each sentence came to me briefly worded, but most expressive ; full of excellent counsel to the boy, tenderly bequeathing " mother and Lizzie " to his care, and bidding him good bye in words the sadder for their simplicity. He added a few lines, with steady hand, and, as I sealed it, said, with a patient sort of sigh, " I hope the answer will come in time for me to see it ;" then, turning away his face, laid the flowers against his lips, as if to hide some quiver of emotion at the thought of such a sudden sundering of all the dear home ties.

These things had happened two days before; now John was dying, and the letter had not come. I had been summoned to many death beds in my life, but to none that made my heart ache as it did then, since my mother called me to watch the departure of a spirit akin to this in its gentleness and patient strength. As I went in, John stretched out both hands:

"I knew you'd come! I guess I'm moving on, ma'am."

He was; and so rapidly that, even while he spoke, over his face I saw the grey veil falling that no human hand can lift. I sat down by him, wiped the drops from his forehead, stirred the air about him with the slow wave of a fan, and waited to help him die. He stood in sore need of help—and I could do so little; for, as the doctor had foretold, the strong body rebelled against death, and fought every inch of the way, forcing him to draw each breath with a spasm, and clench his hands with an imploring look, as if he asked, "How long must I endure this, and be still!" For hours he suffered dumbly, without a moment's respite, or a moment's murmuring; his limbs grew cold, his face damp, his lips white, and, again and again, he tore the covering off his breast, as if the lightest weight added to his agony; yet through it all, his eyes never lost their perfect serenity, and the man's soul seemed to sit therein, undaunted by the ills that vexed his flesh.

One by one, the men woke, and round the room appeared a circle of pale faces and watchful eyes, full of awe and pity; for, though a stranger, John was beloved by all. Each man there had wondered at his patience, respected his piety, admired his fortitude, and now lamented his hard death; for the influence of an upright nature had made itself deeply felt, even in one little week. Presently, the Jonathan who so loved this comely David, came creeping from his bed for a last look and word. The kind soul was full of trouble, as the choke in his voice, the grasp of his hand, betrayed; but there were no tears, and the farewell of the friends was the more touching for its brevity.

" Old boy, how are you?" faltered the one.

" Most through, thank heaven!" whispered the other.

" Can I say or do anything for you anywheres?"

" Take my things home, and tell them that I did my best."

" I will! I will!"

" Good bye, Ned."

" Good bye, John, good bye!"

They kissed each other, tenderly as women, and so parted, for poor Ned could not stay to see his comrade die. For a little while, there was no sound in the room but the drip of water, from a stump or two, and John's distressful gasps, as he slowly breathed his life away. I thought him nearly gone, and had just laid down the fan, believing its help to be no longer needed, when suddenly he rose up in his bed, and cried out with a bitter cry that broke the silence, sharply startling every one with its agonized appeal:

" For God's sake, give me air!"

It was the only cry pain or death had wrung from him, the only boon he had asked; and none of us could grant it, for all the airs that blew were useless now. Dan flung up the window. The first red streak of dawn was warming the grey east, a herald of the coming sun; John saw it, and with the love of light which lingers in us to the end, seemed to read in it a sign of hope of help, for, over his whole face there broke that mysterious expression, brighter than any smile, which

often comes to eyes that look their last. He laid himself
gently down ; and, stretching out his strong right arm, as if to
grasp and bring the blessed air to his lips in a fuller flow,
lapsed into a merciful unconsciousness, which assured us that
for him suffering was forever past. He died then ; for, though
the heavy breaths still tore their way up for a little longer,
they were but the waves of an ebbing tide that beat unfelt
against the wreck, which an immortal voyager had deserted
with a smile. He never spoke again, but to the end held my
hand close, so close that when he was asleep at last, I could
not draw it away. Dan helped me, warning me as he did so
that it was unsafe for dead and living flesh to lie so long
together; but though my hand was strangely cold and stiff,
and four white marks remained across its back, even when
warmth and color had returned elsewhere, I could not but be
glad that, through its touch, the presence of human sympathy,
perhaps, had lightened that hard hour.

When they had made him ready for the grave, John lay in
state for half an hour, a thing which seldom happened in that
busy place ; but a universal sentiment of reverence and
affection seemed to fill the hearts of all who had known or
heard of him ; and when the rumor of his death went through
the house, always astir, many came to see him, and I felt a
tender sort of pride in my lost patient ; for he looked a most
heroic figure, lying there stately and still as the statue of some
young knight asleep upon his tomb. The lovely expression
which so often beautifies dead faces, soon replaced the marks
of pain, and I longed for those who loved him best to see him
when half an hour's acquaintance with Death had made them
friends. As we stood looking at him, the ward master handed
me a letter, saying it had been forgotten the night before. It
was John's letter, come just an hour too late to gladden the

eyes that had longed and looked for it so eagerly! but he had it ; for, after I had cut some brown locks for his mother, and taken off the ring to send her, telling how well the talisman had done its work, I kissed this good son for her sake, and laid the letter in his hand, still folded as when I drew my own away, feeling that its place was there, and making myself happy with the thought, that, even in his solitary grave in the "Government Lot," he would not be without some token of the love which makes life beautiful and outlives death. Then I left him, glad to have known so genuine a man, and carrying with me an enduring memory of the brave Virginia blacksmith, as he lay serenely waiting for the dawn of that long day which knows no night.

CHAPTER V.

OFF DUTY.

" My dear girl, we shall have you sick in your bed, unless you keep yourself warm and quiet for a few days. Widow Wadman can take care of the ward alone, now the men are so comfortable, and have her vacation when you are about again. Now do be prudent in time, and don't let me have to add a Periwinkle to my bouquet of patients."

This advice was delivered, in a paternal manner, by the youngest surgeon in the hospital, a kind-hearted little gentleman, who seemed to consider me a frail young blossom, that needed much cherishing, instead of a stout spinster, who had been knocking about the world for thirty years. At the time I write of, he discovered me sitting on the stairs, with a fine cloud of unwholesome steam rising from the washroom; a party of January breezes disporting themselves in the halls; and perfumes, by no means from " Araby the blest," keeping them company; while I enjoyed a fit of coughing, which caused my head to spin in a way that made the application of a cool banister both necessary and agreeable, as I waited for the frolicsome wind to restore the breath I'd lost; cheering myself, meantime, with a secret conviction that pneumonia was waiting for me round the corner. This piece of advice had been offered by several persons for a week, and refused by me with the obstinacy with which my sex is so richly gifted. But the last few hours had developed several surprising internal and external phenomena, which impressed upon me the fact that if I didn't make a masterly retreat very soon, I should tumble down somewhere, and have to be borne ignominiously from the field. My head felt like a cannon ball; my feet had a tendency to cleave to the floor; the walls at times undulated in a most disagreeable manner; people looked unnaturally big; and the very bottles on the mantle piece appeared to dance derisively before my eyes. Taking these things into consideration, while blinking stupidly at Dr. Z., I resolved to retire gracefully, if I must; so, with a valedictory to my boys, a private lecture to Mrs. Wadman, and a fervent wish that I could take off my body and work in my soul, I mournfully ascended to my apartment, and Nurse P. was reported off duty.

For the benefit of any ardent damsel whose patriotic fancy may have surrounded hospital life with a halo of charms, I will briefly describe the bower to which I retired, in a somewhat ruinous condition. It was well ventilated, for five panes of glass had suffered compound fractures, which all the surgeons and nurses had failed to heal; the two windows were draped with sheets, the church hospital opposite being a brick and mortar Argus, and the female mind cherishing a prejudice in favor of retiracy during the night-capped periods of existence. A bare floor supported two narrow iron beds, spread with thin mattrasses like plasters, furnished with pillows in the last stages of consumption. In a fire place, guiltless of shovel,

tongs, andirons, or grate, burned a log, inch by inch, being too
long to go on all at once; so, while the fire blazed away at one
end, I did the same at the other, as I tripped over it a dozen
times a day, and flew up to poke it a dozen times at night. A
mirror (let us be elegant!) of the dimensions of a muffin,
and about as reflective, hung over a tin basin, blue pitcher,
and a brace of yellow mugs. Two invalid tables, ditto chairs,
wandered here and there, and the closet contained a varied
collection of bonnets, bottles, bags, boots, bread and butter,
boxes and bugs. The closet was a regular Blue Beard
cupboard to me; I always opened it with fear and trembling,
owing to rats, and shut it in anguish of spirit; for time and
space were not to be had, and chaos reigned along with the
rats. Our chimney-piece was decorated with a flat-iron, a
Bible, a candle minus stick, a lavender bottle, a new tin pan,
so brilliant that it served nicely for a pier-glass, and such of
the portly black bugs as preferred a warmer climate than the
rubbish hole afforded. Two arks, commonly called trunks,
lurked behind the door, containing the worldly goods of the
twain who laughed and cried, slept and scrambled, in this
refuge; while from the white-washed walls above either bed,
looked down the pictured faces of those whose memory could
make for us —

" One little room an everywhere."

For a day or two I managed to appear at meals; for the
human grub must eat till the butterfly is ready to break loose,
and no one had time to come up two flights while it was
possible for me to come down. Far be it from me to add
another affliction or reproach to that enduring man, the stew-
ard; for, compared with his predecessor, he was a horn of
plenty; but — I put it to any candid mind — is not the

following bill of fare susceptible of improvement, without plunging the nation madly into debt? The three meals were " pretty much of a muchness," and consisted of beef, evidently put down for the men of '76 ; pork, just in from the street ; army bread, composed of saw-dust and saleratus ; butter, salt as if churned by Lot's wife ; stewed blackberries, so much like preserved cockroaches, that only those devoid of imagination could partake thereof with relish ; coffee, mild and muddy ; tea, three dried huckleberry leaves to a quart of water — flavored with lime — also animated and unconscious of any approach to clearness. Variety being the spice of life, a small pinch of the article would have been appreciated by the hungry, hard-working sisterhood, one of whom, though accustomed to plain fare, soon found herself reduced to bread and water ; having an inborn repugnance to the fat of the land, and the salt of the earth.

Another peculiarity of these hospital meals was the rapidity with which the edibles vanished, and the impossibility of getting a drop or crumb after the usual time. At the first ring of the bell, a general stampede took place ; some twenty hungry souls rushed to the dining-room, swept over the table like a swarm of locusts, and left no fragment for any tardy creature who arrived fifteen minutes late. Thinking it of more importance that the patients should be well and comfortably fed, I took my time about my own meals for the first day or two after I came, but was speedily enlightened by Isaac, the black waiter, who bore with me a few times, and then informed me, looking as stern as fate :

" I say, mam, ef you comes so late you can't have no vittles, — 'cause I'm 'bleeged fer ter git things ready fer de doctors 'mazin' spry arter you nusses and folks is done. De gen'lemen don't kere fer ter wait, no more does I ; so you jes' please ter come at de time, and dere won't be no frettin' nowheres."

It was a new sensation to stand looking at a full table, painfully conscious of one of the vacuums which Nature abhors, and receive orders to right about face, without partaking of the nourishment which your inner woman clam. orously demanded. The doctors always fared better than we ; and for a moment a desperate impulse prompted me to give them a hint, by walking off with the mutton, or confiscating the pie. But Ike's eye was on me, and, to my shame be it spoken. I walked meekly away ; went dinnerless that day, and that evening went to market, laying in a small stock of crackers, cheese and apples, that my boys might not be neglected, nor myself obliged to bolt solid and liquid dyspepsias, or starve. This plan would have succeeded admirably had not the evil star under which I was born, been in the ascendant during that month, and cast its malign influences even into my " 'umble " larder ; for the rats had their dessert off my cheese, the bugs set up housekeeping in my cracker-bag. and the apples like all worldly riches, took to themselves wings and flew away ; whither no man could tell, though certain black imps might have thrown light upon the matter, had not the plaintiff in the case been loth to add another to the many trials of long-suffering Africa. After this failure I resigned myself to fate, and, remembering that bread was called the staff of life, leaned pretty exclusively upon it ; but it proved a broken reed, and I came to the ground after a few weeks of prison fare, varied by an occasional potato or surreptitious sip of milk.

Very soon after leaving the care of my ward, I discovered that I had no appetite, and cut the bread and butter interests almost entirely, trying the exercise and sun cure instead.

Flattering myself that I had plenty of time, and could see all that was to be seen, so far as a lone lorn female could venture in a city, one-half of whose male population seemed to be taking the other half to the guard-house. — every morning I took a brisk run in one direction or another ; for the January days were as mild as Spring. A rollicking north wind and occasional snow storm would have been more to my taste, for the one would have braced and refreshed tired body and soul, the other have purified the air, and spread a clean coverlid over the bed, wherein the capital of these United States appeared to be dozing pretty soundly just then.

One of these trips was to the Armory Hospital, the neatness, comfort, and convenience of which makes it an honor to its presiding genius, and arouses all the covetous propensities of such nurses as came from other hospitals to visit it.

The long, clean, warm, and airy wards, built barrack-fashion, with the nurse's room at the end, were fully appreciated by Nurse Periwinkle, whose ward and private bower were cold, dirty, inconvenient, up stairs and down stairs, and in everybody's chamber. At the Armory, in ward K, I found a cheery, bright-eyed, white-aproned little lady, reading at her post near the stove ; matting under her feet ; a draft of fresh air flowing in above her head ; a table full of trays, glasses, and such matters, on one side, a large, well-stocked medicine chest on the other; and all her duty seemed to be going about now and then to give doses, issue orders, which well-trained attendants executed, and pet, advise, or comfort Tom, Dick, or Harry, as she found best. As I watched the proceedings, I recalled my own tribulations, and contrasted the two hospitals in a way that would have caused my summary dismissal, could it have been reported at headquarters. Here, order, method, common sense and liberality seemed to rule in a style

that did one's heart good to see ; at the Hurly burly Hotel,
disorder, discomfort, bad management, and no visible head,
reduced things to a condition which I despair of describing.
The circumlocution fashion prevailed, forms and fusses tormented our souls, and unnecessary strictness in one place was
counterbalanced by unpardonable laxity in another.   Here is
a sample : I am dressing Sam Dammer's shoulder ; and, having
cleansed the wound, look about for some strips of adhesive
plaster to hold on the little square of wet linen which is to
cover the gunshot wound ; the case is not in the tray ; Frank,
the sleepy, half-sick attendant, knows nothing of it ; we
rummage high and low ; Sam is tired, and fumes ; Frank
dawdles and yawns ; the men advise and laugh at the flurry ;
I feel like a boiling tea-kettle, with the lid ready to fly off and
damage somebody.

  " Go and borrow some from the next ward, and spend the
rest of the day in finding ours," I finally command.   A pause ;
then Frank scuffles back with the message : " Miss Peppercorn
ain't got none, and says you ain't no business to lose your own
duds and go borrowin' other folkses."   I say nothing, for fear
of saying too much, but fly to the surgery.   Mr. Toddypestle
informs me that I can't have anything without an order from
the surgeon of my ward.   Great heavens ! where is he ? and
away I rush, up and down, here and there, till at last I find
him, in a state of bliss over a complicated amputation, in the
fourth story.   I make my demand ; he answers : " In five
minutes," and works away, with his head upside down, as he
ties an artery, saws a bone, or does a little needle-work, with
a visible relish and very sanguinary pair of hands.   The five
minutes grow to fifteen, and Frank appears, with the remark
that, " Dammer wants to know what in thunder you are
keeping him there with his finger on a wet rag for ?"   Dr. P.

tears himself away long enough to scribble the order, with which I plunge downward to the surgery again, find the door locked, and, while hammering away on it, am told that two friends are waiting to see me in the hall. The matron being away, her parlor is locked, and there is no where to see my guests but in my own room, and no time to enjoy them till the plaster is found. I settle this matter, and circulate through the house to find Toddypestle, who has no right to leave the surgery till night. He is discovered in the dead house, smoking a cigar, and very much the worse for his researches among the spirituous preparations that fill the surgery shelves. He is inclined to be gallant, and puts the finishing blow to the fire of my wrath; for the tea-kettle lid flies off, and driving him before me to his post, I fling down the order, take what I choose; and, leaving the absurd incapable kissing his hand to me, depart, feeling as Grandma Riglesty is reported to have done, when she vainly sought for chips, in Bimleck Jackwood's " shif less paster."

I find Dammer a well acted charade of his own name, and, just as I get him done, struggling the while with a burning desire to clap an adhesive strip across his mouth, full of heaven-defying oaths, Frank takes up his boot to put it on, and exclaims :

" I'm blest ef here ain't that case now ! I recollect seeing it fall in this mornin', but forgot all about it, till my heel went smash inter it. Here, ma'am, ketch hold on it, and give the boys a sheet on't all round, 'gainst it tumbles inter t'other boot next time yer want it."

If a look could annihilate, Francis Saucebox would have ceased to exist; but it couldn't ; therefore, he yet lives, to aggravate some unhappy woman's soul, and wax fat in some equally congenial situation.

Now, while I'm freeing my mind, I should like to enter my protest against employing convalescents as attendants, instead of strong, properly trained, and cheerful men. How it may be in other places I cannot say; but here it was a source of constant trouble and confusion, these feeble, ignorant men trying to sweep, scrub, lift, and wait upon their sicker comrades. One, with a diseased heart, was expected to run up and down stairs, carry heavy trays, and move helpless men; he tried it, and grew rapidly worse than when he first came: and, when he was ordered out to march away to the convalescent hospital, fell, in a sort of fit, before he turned the corner, and was brought back to die. Another, hurt by a fall from his horse, endeavored to do his duty, but failed entirely, and the wrath of the ward master fell upon the nurse, who must either scrub the rooms herself, or take the lecture; for the boy looked stout and well, and the master never happened to see him turn white with pain, or hear him groan in his sleep when an involuntary motion strained his poor back. Constant complaints were being made of incompetent attendants, and some dozen women did double duty, and then were blamed for breaking down. If any hospital director fancies this a good and economical arrangement, allow one used up nurse to tell him it isn't, and beg him to spare the sisterhood, who sometimes, in their sympathy, forget that they are mortal, and run the risk of being made immortal, sooner than is agreeable to their partial friends.

Another of my few rambles took me to the Senate Chamber, hoping to hear and see if this large machine was run any better than some small ones I knew of. I was too late, and found the Speaker's chair occupied by a colored gentleman of ten; while two others were on their legs, having a hot debate on the cornball question, as they gathered the waste paper strewn about the floor into bags; and several white members played leap-frog over the desks, a much wholesomer relaxation than some of the older Senators indulge in, I fancy. Finding the coast clear, I likewise gambolled up and down, from gallery to gallery; sat in Sumner's chair, and cudgelled an imaginary Brooks within an inch of his life; examined Wilson's books in the coolest possible manner; warmed my feet at one of the national registers; read people's names on scattered envelopes, and pocketed a castaway autograph or two; watched the somewhat unparliamentary proceedings going on about me, and wondered who in the world all the sedate gentlemen were, who kept popping out of odd doors here and there, like respectable Jacks-in-the-box. Then I wandered over the palatial residence of Mrs. Columbia, and examined its many beauties, though I can't say I thought her a tidy housekeeper, and didn't admire her taste in pictures, for the eye of this humble individual soon wearied of expiring patriots, who all appeared to be quitting their earthly tabernacles in convulsious, ruffled shirts, and a whirl of torn banners bomb shells, and buff and blue arms and legs.

The statuary also was massive and concrete, but rather wearying to examine; for the colossal ladies and gentlemen carried no cards of introduction in face or figure; so whether the meditative party in a kilt, with well-developed legs, shoes like army slippers, and a ponderous nose, was Columbus, Cato, or Cockelorum Tibby the tragedian, was more than I could tell. Several robust ladies attracted me; but which was America and which Pocahontas was a mystery; for all affected much looseness of costume, dishevelment of hair, swords, arrows, lances scales, and other ornaments quite *passé* with damsels of our day, whose effigies should go down to posterity armed

with fans, crochet needles, riding whips, and parasols, with
here and there one holding pen or pencil, rolling-pin or broom.
The statue of Liberty I recognized at once, for it had no
pedestal as yet, but stood flat in the mud, with Young America
most symbolically making dirt pies, and chip forts, in its
shadow. But high above the squabbling little throng and
their petty plans, the sun shone full on Liberty's broad
forehead, and, in her hand, some summer bird had built its
nest. I accepted the good omen then, and, on the first of
January, the Emancipation Act gave the statue a nobler and
more enduring pedestal than any marble or granite ever carved
and quarried by human hands.

One. trip to Georgetown Heights, where cedars sighed over-
head, dead leaves rustled underfoot, pleasant paths led up and
down, and a brook wound like a silver snake by the blackened
ruins of some French Minister's house, through the poor
gardens of the black washerwomen who congregated there,
and, passing the cemetery with a murmurous lullaby, rolled
away to pay its little tribute to the river. This breezy run
was the last I took ; for, on the morrow, came rain and wind :
and confinement soon proved a powerful reinforcement to the
enemy, who was quietly preparing to spring a mine, and blow
me five hundred miles from the position I had taken in what I
called my Chickahominy Swamp.

Shut up in my room, with no voice, spirits, or books, that
week was not a holiday. by any means. Finding meals a
humbug, I stopped away altogether, trusting that if this sparrow
was of any worth, the Lord would not let it fall to the ground.
Like a flock of friendly ravens, my sister nurses fed me, not
only with food for the body, but kind words for the mind ;
and soon, from being half starved, I found myself so beteaed
and betoasted, petted and served, that I was nearly killed

with kindness, in spite of cough, headache, a painful conscious ness of my pleura, and a realizing sense of bones in the human frame. From the pleasant house on the hill, the home in the heart of Washington, and the Willard caravansary, came friends new and old, with bottles, baskets, carriages and invitations for the invalid ; and daily our Florence Nightingale climbed the steep stairs, stealing a moment from her busy life, to watch over the stranger, of whom she was as thoughtfully tender as any mother. Long may she wave ! Whatever others may think or say, Nurse Periwinkle is forever grateful ; and among her relics of that Washington defeat, none is more valued than the little book which appeared on her pillow, one dreary day ; for the D D. written in it means to her far more than Doctor of Divinity.

Being forbidden to meddle with fleshly arms and legs, I solaced myself by mending cotton ones, and, as I sat sewing at my window, watched the moving panorama that passed below ; amusing myself with taking notes of the most striking figures in it. Long trains of army wagons kept up a perpetual rumble from morning till night ; ambulances rattled to and fro with busy surgeons, nurses taking an airing, or convalescents going in parties to be fitted to artificial limbs. Strings of sorry looking horses passed, saying as plainly as dumb creatures could, "Why, in a city full of them, is there no *horse*pital for us ?" Often a cart came by, with several rough coffins in it and no mourners following ; barouches, with invalid officers, rolled round the corner, and carriage loads of pretty children, with black coachmen, footmen, and maids. The women who took their walks abroad, were so extinguished in three story bonnets, with overhanging balconies of flowers, that their charms were obscured ; and all I can say of them is, that they dressed in the worst possible taste, and walked like ducks.

The men did the picturesque, and did it so well that Washington looked like a mammoth masquerade. Spanish hats, scarlet lined riding cloaks, swords and sashes, high boots and bright spurs, beards and mustaches, which made plain faces comely, and comely faces heroic; these vanities of the flesh transformed our butchers, bakers, and candlestick makers into gallant riders of gaily caparisoned horses, much handsomer than themselves; and dozens of such figures were constantly prancing by, with private prickings of spurs, for the benefit of the perambulating flower-bed. Some of these gentlemen affected painfully tight uniforms, and little caps, kept on by some new law of gravitation, as they covered only the bridge of the nose, yet never fell off; the men looked like stuffed fowls, and rode as if the safety of the nation depended on their speed alone. The fattest, greyest officers dressed most, and ambled statelily along, with orderlies behind, trying to look as if they didn't know the stout party in front, and doing much caracoling on their own account.

The mules were my especial delight; and an hour's study of a constant succession of them introduced me to many of their characteristics; for six of these odd little beasts drew each army wagon, and went hopping like frogs through the stream of mud that gently rolled along the street. The coquettish mule had small feet. a nicely trimmed tassel of a tail, perked up ears, and seemed much given to little tosses of the head, affected skips and prances; and, if he wore the bells, or were bedizzened with a bit of finery, put on as many airs as any belle. The moral mule was a stout, hard-working creature, always tugging with all his might; often pulling away after the rest had stopped, laboring under the conscientious delusion that food for the entire army depended upon his private exertions. I respected this style of mule; and, had

I possessed a juicy cabbage, would have pressed it upon him, with thanks for his excellent example. The historical mule was a melo-dramatic quadruped, prone to startling humanity by erratic leaps, and wild plunges, much shaking of his stubborn head, and lashing out of his vicious heels ; now and then falling flat, and apparently dying *a la* Forrest : a gasp — a squirm — a flop, and so on, till the street was well blocked up, the drivers all swearing like demons in bad hats, and the chief actor's circulation decidedly quickened by every variety of kick, cuff, jerk and haul. When the last breath seemed to have left his body, and " Doctors were in vain," a sudden resurrection took place ; and if ever a mule laughed with scornful triumph, that was the beast, as he leisurely rose, gave a comfortable shake ; and, calmly regarding the excited crowd seeemed to say — " A hit ! a decided hit ! for the stupidest of animals has bamboozled a dozen men. Now, then ! what are *you* stopping the way for ?" The pathetic mule was, perhaps, the most interesting of all ; for, though he always seemed to be the smallest, thinnest, weakest of the six, the postillion, with big boots, long-tailed coat, and heavy whip, was sure to bestride this one, who struggled feebly along, head down, coat muddy and rough, eye spiritless and sad, his very tail a mortified stump, and the whole beast a picture of meek misery, fit to touch a heart of stone. The jovial mule was a roly poly, happy-go-lucky little piece of horse-flesh, taking everything easily, from cudgeling to caressing ; strolling along with a roguish twinkle of the eye, and, if the thing were possible, would have had his hands in his pockets, and whistled as he went. If there ever chanced to be an apple core, a stray turnip, or wisp of hay, in the gutter, this Mark Tapley was sure to find it, and none of his mates seemed to begrudge him his bite. I suspected this fellow was the peacemaker,

shadow of Father Abraham, I had endeavored to walk discreetly, and curb my unruly member; looking about me with all my eyes the while, and saving up the result of my observations for future use. I had not been there a week before the neglected, devil-may care expression in many of the faces about me, seemed an urgent appeal to leave nursing white bodies, and take some care for these black souls. Much as the lazy boys and saucy girls tormented me, I liked them, and found that any show of interest or friendliness brought out the better traits which live in the most degraded and forsaken of us all. I liked their cheerfulness, for the dreariest old hag, who scrubbed all day in that pestilential steam, gossipped and grinned all the way out, when night set her free from drudgery. The girls romped with their dusky sweethearts, or tossed their babies, with the tender pride that makes mother-love a beautifier to the homeliest face. The men and boys sang and whistled all day long; and often. as I held my watch, the silence of the night was sweetly broken by some chorus from the street, full of real melody, whether the song was of heaven, or of hoe-cakes ; and, as I listened, I felt that we never should doubt nor despair concerning a race which, through such griefs and wrongs, still clings to this good gift, and seems to solace with it the patient hearts that wait and watch and hope until the end.

I expected to have to defend myself from accusations of a prejudice against color; but was surprised to find things just the other way, and daily shocked some neighbor by treating the blacks as I did the whites. The men *would* swear at the " darkies," would put two *gs* into negro, and scoff at the idea of any good coming from such trash. The nurses were willing to be served by the colored people, but seldom thanked them, never praised, and scarcely recognized them in the street ;

whereat the blood of two generations of abolitionists waxed hot in my veins, and, at the first opportunity, proclaimed itself, and asserted the right of free speech as doggedly as the irrepressible Folsom herself.

Happening to catch up a funny little black baby, who was toddling about the nurses' kitchen, one day, when I went down to make a mess for some of my men, a Virginia woman standing by elevated her most prominent feature, with a sniff of disapprobation, exclaiming :

" Gracious, Miss P. ! how can you ? I've been here six months, and never so much as touched the little toad with a poker."

" More shame for you, ma'am," responded Miss P. ; and, with the natural perversity of a Yankee, followed up the blow by kissing " the toad," with ardor. His face was providentially as clean and shiny as if his mamma had just polished it up with a corner of her apron and a drop from the tea-kettle spout, like old Aunt Chloe, This rash act, and the antislavery lecture that followed, while one hand stirred gruel for sick America, and the other hugged baby Africa, did not produce the cheering result which I fondly expected ; for my comrade henceforth regarded me as a dangerous fanatic, and my protegé nearly came to his death by insisting on swarming up stairs to my room, on all occasions, and being walked on like a little black spider.

I waited for New Year's day with more eagerness than I had ever known before ; and, though it brought me no gift, I felt rich in the act of justice so tardily performed toward some of those about me. As the bells rung midnight, I electrified my room-mate by dancing out of bed, throwing up the window, and flapping my handkerchief, with a feeble cheer, in answer to the shout of a group of colored men in the street below. All night they tooted and tramped, fired crackers, sung " Glory, Hallelujah," and took comfort, poor souls ! in their own way. The sky was clear, the moon shone benignly, a mild wind blew across the river, and all good omens seemed to usher in the dawn of the day whose noontide cannot now be long in coming. If the colored people had taken hands and danced around the White House, with a few cheers for the much abused gentleman who has immortalized himself by one just act, no President could have had a finer levee, or one to be prouder of.

While these sights and sounds were going on without, curious scenes were passing within, and I was learning that one of the best methods of fitting oneself to be a nurse in a hospital, is to be a patient there. For then only can one wholly realize what the men suffer and sigh for ; how acts of kindness touch and win ; how much or little we are to those about us ; and for the first time really see that in coming there we have taken our lives in our hands, and may have to pay dearly for a brief experience. Every one was very kind ; the attendants of my ward often came up to report progress, to fill my wood-box, or bring messages and presents from my boys. The nurses took many steps with those tired feet of theirs, and several came each evening, to chat over my fire and make things cosy for the night. The doctors paid daily visits, tapped at my lungs to see if pneumonia was within, left doses without names, and went away, leaving me as ignorant, and much more uncomfortable than when they came. Hours began to get confused ; people looked odd ; queer faces haunted the room, and the nights were one long fight with weariness and pain. Letters from home grew anxious ; the doctors lifted their eyebrows, and nodded ominously ; friends said " Don't stay," and an internal rebellion seconded the advice ;

but the three months were not out, and the idea of giving up so soon was proclaiming a defeat before I was fairly routed ; so to all " Don't stays " I opposed " I wills," till, one fine morning, a gray-headed gentleman rose like a welcome ghost on my hearth ; and, at the sight of him, my resolution melted away, my heart turned traitor to my boys, and, when he said, " Come home," I answered, " Yes, father ;" and so ended my career as an army nurse.

I never shall regret the going, though a sharp tussle with typhoid, ten dollars, and a wig, are all the visible results of the experiment ; for one may live and learn much in a month. A good fit of illness proves the value of health ; real danger tries one's mettle ; and self-sacrifice sweetens character. Let no one who sincerely desires to help the work on in this way, delay going through any fear ; for the worth of life lies in the experiences that fill it, and this is one which cannot be forgotten. All that is best and bravest in the hearts of men and women, comes out in scenes like these ; and, though a hospital is a rough school, its lessons are both stern and salutary ; and the humblest of pupils there, in proportion to his faithfulness, learns a deeper faith in God and in himself. I, for one, would return tomorrow, on the "up-again,-and-take-another " principle, if I could ; for the amount of pleasure and profit I got out of that month compensates for all after pangs ; and, though a sadly womanish feeling, I take some satisfaction in the thought that, if I could not lay my head on the altar of my country, I have my hair ; and that is more than handsome Helen did for her dead husband, when she sacrificed only the ends of her ringlets on his urn. Therefore, I close this little chapter of hospital experiences, with the regret that they were no better worth recording ; and add the poetical gem with which I console myself for the untimely demise of "Nurse Periwinkle :"

> Oh, lay her in a little pit,
> With a marble stone to cover it;
> And carve thereon a gruel spoon,
> To show a "nuss" has died too soon.

CHAPTER VI.

A POSTSCRIPT.

My Dear S. : — As inquiries like your own have come to me from various friendly readers of the Sketches, I will answer them *en masse*, and in printed form, as a sort of postscript to what has gone before. One of these questions was, " Are there no services by hospital death-beds, or on Sundays ?"

In most Hospitals I hope there are ; in ours, the men died, and were carried away, with as little ceremony as on a battle-field. The first event of this kind which I witnessed was so very brief, and bare of anything like reverence, sorrow, or pious consolation, that I heartily agreed with the bluntly expressed opinion of a Maine man lying next his comrade, who died with no visible help near him, but a compassionate woman and a tender-hearted Irishman, who dropped upon his knees, and told his beads, with Catholic fervor, for the **good** of his Protestant brother's parting soul :

" If, after gettin' all the hard knocks, we are left to die

this way, with nothing but a Paddy's prayers to help us, I guess Christians are rather scarce round Washington."

I thought so too ; but though Miss Blank, one of my mates, anxious that souls should be ministered to, as well as bodies, spoke more than once to the Chaplain, nothing ever came cf it. Unlike another Shepherd, whose earnest piety weekly purified the Senate Chamber, this man did not feed as well as fold his flock, nor make himself a human symbol of the Divine Samaritan, who never passes by on the other side.

I have since learned that our non-commital Chaplain had been a Professor in some Southern College ; and, though he maintained that he had no secesh proclivities, I can testify that he sceded from his ministerial duties, I may say, ske-daddled ; for, being one of his own words, it is as appropriate as inelegant. He read Emerson, quoted Carlyle, and tried to be a Chaplain ; but, judging from his success, I am afraid he still hankered after the hominy pots of Rebeldom.

Occasionally, on a Sunday afternoon, such of the nurses, officers, attendants, and patients as could avail themselves of it, were gathered in the Ball Room, for an hour's service, of which the singing was the better part. To me it seemed that if ever strong, wise, and loving words were needed, it was then ; if ever mortal man had living texts before his eyes to illustrate and illuminate his thought, it was there ; and if ever hearts were prompted to devoutest self-abnegation, it was in the work which brought us to anything but a Chapel of Ease. But some spiritual paralysis seemed to have befallen our pastor ; for, though many faces turned toward him, full of the dumb hunger that often comes to men when suffering or danger brings them nearer to the heart of things, they were offered the chaff of divinity, and its wheat was left for less needy gleaners, who knew where to look. Even the fine old Bible stories, which may be made as lifelike as any history of our day, by a vivid fancy and pictorial diction, were robbed of all their charms by dry explanations and literal applications, instead of being useful and pleasant lessons to those men, whom weakness had rendered as docile as children in a father's hands.

I watched the listless countenances all about me, while we listened to a dull sermon, delivered with a monotonous tone, a business-like manner, and a very visible desire to get the uninteresting job done as expeditiously as possible; which demonstrations were most successful in making the Sunday services a duty, not a pleasure. Listless they were at the beginning, and listless at the end; but the instant some stirring old hymn was given out, sleepy eyes brightened, lounging figures sat erect, and many a poor lad rose up in his bed, or stretched an eager hand for the book, while all broke out with a heartiness that proved that somewhere at the core of even the most abandoned, there still glowed some remnant of the native piety that flows in music from the heart of every little child. Even the big rebel joined, and boomed away in a thunderous bass, singing —

    " Salvation! let the echoes fly,"

as energetically as if he felt the need of a speedy execution of the command.

That was the pleasantest moment of the hour, for then it seemed a homelike and happy spot; the groups of men looking over one another's shoulders as they sang; the few silent figures in the beds; here and there a woman noiselessly performing some necessary duty, and singing as she worked;

while in the arm chair standing in the midst, I placed, for my own satisfaction, the imaginary likeness of a certain faithful pastor, who took all outcasts by the hand, smote the devil in whatever guise he came, and comforted the indigent in spirit with the best wisdom of a great and tender heart, which still speaks to us from its Italian grave. With that addition, my picture was complete; and I often longed to take a veritable sketch of a Hospital Sunday, for, despite its drawbacks, consisting of continued labor, the want of proper books, the barren preaching that bore no fruit, this day was never like the other six.

True to their home training, our New England boys did their best to make it what it should be. With many, there was much reading of Testaments, humming over of favorite hymns, and looking at such books as I could cull from a miscellaneous library. Some lay idle, slept, or gossiped; yet, when I came to them for a quiet evening chat or reading, they often talked freely and well of themselves; would blunder out some timid hope that their troubles might "do 'em good, and keep 'em stiddy;" would choke a little, as they said good night, and turned their faces to the wall to think of mother, wife, or home, these human ties seeming to be the most vital religion which they yet knew. I observed that some of them did not wear their caps on this day, though at other times they clung to them like Quakers; wearing them in bed, putting them on to read the paper, eat an apple, or write a letter, as if, like a new sort of Samson, their strength lay, not in their hair, but in their hats. Many read no novels, swore less, were more silent, orderly, and cheerful, as if the Lord were an invisible Ward-master, who went his rounds but once a week, and must find all things at their best. I liked all this in the poor, rough boys, and could have found it in my heart to put down sponge and tea-pot, and preach a little sermon then and there, while homesickness and pain had made these natures soft, that some good seed might be cast therein, to blossom and bear fruit here or hereafter.

Regarding the admission of friends to nurse their sick, I can only say, it was not allowed at Hurlyburly House ; though one indomitable parent took my ward by storm, and held her position, in spite of doctors, matron, and Nurse Periwinkle Though it was against the rules, though the culprit was an acid, frost-bitten female, though the young man would have done quite as well without her anxious fussiness, and the whole room-full been much more comfortable, there was something so irresistible in this persistent devotion, that no one had the heart to oust her from her post. She slept on the floor, without uttering a complaint ; bore jokes somewhat of the rudest ; fared scantily, though her basket was daily filled with luxuries for her boy ; and tended that petulant personage with a never-failing patience beautiful to see.

I feel a glow of moral rectitude in saying this of her ; for, though a perfect pelican to her young, she pecked and cackled (I don't know that pelicans usually express their emotions in that manner,) most obstreperously, when others invaded her premises ; and led me a weary life, with " George's tea-rusks," " George's foot-bath," " George's measles," and " George's mother ;" till, after a sharp passage of arms and tongues with the matron, she wrathfully packed up her rusks, her son, and herself, and departed, in an ambulance, scolding to the very last.

This is the comic side of the matter. The serious one is harder to describe ; for the presence, however brief, of relations and friends by the bedsides of the dead or dying, is always a trial to the bystanders. They are not near enough to know how best to comfort, yet too near to turn their backs upon the sorrow that finds its only solace in listening to recitals of last words, breathed into nurse's ears, or receiving the tender legacies of love and longing bequeathed through them.

To me, the saddest sight I saw in that sad place, was the spectacle of a grey-haired father, sitting hour after hour by his son, dying from the poison of his wound. The old father, hale and hearty; the young son, past all help, though one could scarcely believe it; for the subtle fever, burning his strength away, flushed his cheeks with color, filled his eyes with lustre, and lent a mournful mockery of health to face and figure, making the poor lad comelier in death than in life. His bed was not in my ward; but I was often in and out, and, for a day or two, the pair were much together, saying little, but looking much. The old man tried to busy himself with book or pen, that his presence might not be a burden; and once, when he sat writing, to the anxious mother at home, doubtless, I saw the son's eyes fixed upon his face, with a look of mingled resignation and regret, as if endeavoring to teach himself to say cheerfully the long good bye. And again, when the son slept, the father watched him, as he had himself been watched; and though no feature of his grave countenance changed, the rough hand, smoothing the lock of hair upon the pillow, the bowed attitude of the grey head, were more pathetic than the loudest lamentations. The son died; and the father took home the pale relic of the life he gave, offering a little money to the nurse, as the only visible return it was in his power to make her; for, though very grateful, he was poor. Of course, she did not take it, but found a richer compensation in the old man's earnest declaration:

"My boy couldn't have been better cared for if he'd been at home ; and God will reward you for it, though I can't."

My own experiences of this sort began when my first man died. He had scarcely been removed, when his wife came in. Her eye went straight to the well-known bed ; it was empty ; and feeling, yet not believing the hard truth, she cried out, with a look I never shall forget :

" Why, where's Emanuel ?"

I had never seen her before, did not know her relationship to the man whom I had only nursed for a day, and was about to tell her he was gone, when McGee, the tender-hearted Irishman before mentioned, brushed by me with a cheerful — " It's shifted to a better bed he is, Mrs. Connel. Come out, dear, till I show ye ;" and, taking her gently by the arm, he led her to the matron, who broke the heavy tidings to the wife, and comforted the widow.

Another day, running up to my room for a breath of fresh air and a five minutes' rest after a disagreeable task, I found a stout young woman sitting on my bed, wearing the miserable look which I had learned to know by that time. Seeing her, reminded me that I had heard of some one's dying in the night, and his sister's arriving in the morning. This must be she, I thought. I pitied her with all my heart. What could I say or do ? Words always seem impertinent at such times ; I did not know the man ; the woman was neither interesting in herself nor graceful in her grief ; yet, having known a sister's sorrow myself, I could not leave her alone with her trouble in that strange place, without a word. So, feeling heart-sick, home-sick, and not knowing what else to do, I just put my arms about her, and began to cry in a very helpless but hearty way ; for, as I seldom indulge in this moist luxury, I like to enjoy it with all my might, when I do.

It so happened I could not have done a better thing; for, though not a word was spoken, each felt the other's sympathy; and, in the silence, our handkerchiefs were more eloquent than words. She soon sobbed herself quiet; and, leaving her on my bed, I went back to work, feeling much refreshed by the shower, though I'd forgotten to rest, and had washed my face instead of my hands. I mention this successful experiment as a receipt proved and approved, for the use of any nurse who may find herself called upon to minister to these wounds of the heart. They will find it more efficacious than cups of tea, smelling-bottles, psalms, or sermons; for a friendly touch and a companionable cry, unite the consolations of all the rest for womankind; and, if genuine, will be found a sovereign cure for the first sharp pang so many suffer in these heavy times.

I am gratified to find that my little Sergeant has found favor in several quarters, and gladly respond to sundry calls for news of him, though my personal knowledge ended five months ago. Next to my good John — I hope the grass is green above him, far away there in Virginia! — I placed the Sergeant on my list of worthy boys; and many a jovial chat have I enjoyed with the merry-hearted lad, who had a fancy for fun, when his poor arm was dressed. While Dr. P. poked and strapped, I brushed the remains of the Sergeant's brown mane — shorn sorely against his will — and gossiped with all my might, the boy making odd faces, exclamations, and appeals, when nerves got the better of nonsense, as they sometimes did:

"I'd rather laugh than cry, when I must sing out anyhow, so just say that bit from Dickens again, please, and I'll stand it like a man." He did; for "Mrs. Cluppins," "Chadband," and "Sam Weller," always helped him through:

thereby causing me to lay another offering of love and admiration on the shrine of the god of my idolatry, though he does
wear too much jewelry and talk slang.

The Sergeant also originated, I believe, the fashion of calling
his neighbors by their afflictions instead of their names ; and I
was rather taken aback by hearing them bandy remarks of
this sort, with perfect good humor and much enjoyment of the
new game.

"Hallo, old Fits is off again !" "How are you, Rheuma-
tiz ?"   "Will you trade apples, Ribs ?"   "I say, Miss P.,
may I give Typus a drink of this ?"   "Look here, No Toes,
lend us a stamp, there's a good feller," etc. He himself was
christened "Baby B.," because he tended his arm on a little
pillow, and called it his infant.

Very fussy about his food was Sergeant B., and much
trotting of attendants was necessary when he partook of nourishment.   Anything more irresistibly wheedlesome I never
saw, and constantly found myself indulging him, like the most
weak-minded parent, merely for the pleasure of seeing his
blue eyes twinkle, his merry mouth break into a smile, and
his one hand execute a jaunty little salute that was entirely
captivating.   I am afraid that Nurse P. damaged her dignity,
frolicking with this persuasive young gentleman, though done
for his well-being.   But "boys will be boys," is perfectly
applicable to the case ; for, in spite of years, sex, and the
"prunes-and-prisms" doctrine laid down for our use, I have
a fellow feeling for lads, and always owed Fate a grudge
because I wasn't a lord of creation instead of a lady.

Since I left, I have heard, from a reliable source, that my
Sergeant has gone home ; therefore, the small romance that
budded the first day I saw him, has blossomed into its second
chapter , and I now imagine "dearest Jane " filling my place,

tending the wounds I tended, brushing the curly jungle I brushed, loving the excellent little youth I loved, and eventually walking altarward, with the Sergeant stumping gallantly at her side. If she doesn't do all this, and no end more, I'll never forgive her; and sincerely pray to the guardian saint of lovers, that "Baby B" may prosper in his wooing, and his name be long in the land.

One of the lively episodes of hospital life, is the frequent marching away of such as are well enough to rejoin their regiments, or betake themselves to some convalescent camp. The ward master comes to the door of each room that is to be thinned, reads off a list of names, bids their owners look sharp and be ready when called for; and, as he vanishes, the rooms fall into an indescribable state of topsy-turvyness, as the boys begin to black their boots, brighten spurs, brush clothes, overhaul knapsacks, make presents; are fitted out with needfuls, and — well, why not? — kissed sometimes, as they say, good by; for in all human probability we shall never meet again, and a woman's heart yearns over anything that has clung to her for help and comfort. I never liked these breakings-up of my little household: though my short stay showed me but three. I was immensely gratified by the hand shakes I got, for their somewhat painful cordiality assured me that I had not tried in vain. The big Prussian rumbled out his unintelligible *adieux*, with a grateful face and a premonitory smooth of his yellow moustache, but got no farther, for some ene else stepped up, with a large brown hand extended, and this recommendation of our very faulty establishment :

" We're off, ma'am, and I'm powerful sorry, for I'd no idea a 'orspittle was such a jolly place. Hope I'll git another ball somewheres easy, so I'll come back, and be took care on again. Mean, ain't it?"

I didn't think so, but the doctrine of inglorious ease was not the the right one to preach up, so I tried to look shocked, failed signally, and consoled myself by giving him the fat pincushion he had admired as the "cutest little machine agoin." Then they fell into line in front of the house, looking rather wan and feeble, some of them, but trying to step out smartly and march in good order, though half the knapsacks were carried by the guard, and several leaned on sticks instead of shouldering guns. All looked up and smiled, or waved heir hands and touched their caps, as they passed under our windows down the long street, and so away, some to their homes in this world, and some to that in the next; and, for the rest of the day, I felt like Rachel mourning for her children, when I saw the empty beds and missed the familiar faces.

You ask if nurses are obliged to witness amputations and such matters, as a part of their duty? I think not, unless they wish; for the patient is under the effects of ether, and needs no care but such as the surgeons can best give. Our work begins afterward, when the poor soul comes to himself, sick, faint, and wandering; full of strange pains and confused visions, of disagreeable sensations and sights. Then we must sooth and sustain, tend and watch; preaching and practicing patience, till sleep and time have restored courage and self-control.

I witnessed several operations; for the height of my ambition was to go to the front after a battle, and feeling that the sooner I inured myself to trying sights, the more useful I should be. Several of my mates shrunk from such things; for though the spirit was wholly willing, the flesh was inconveniently weak. One funereal lady came to try her powers as a nurse ; but, a brief conversation eliciting the facts that she fainted at the sight of blood, was afraid to watch alone, couldn't possibly take care of delirious persons, was nervous about infections, and unable to bear much fatigue, she was mildly dismissed. I hope she found her sphere, but fancy a comfortable bandbox on a high shelf would best meet the requirements of her case.

Dr. Z. suggested that I should witness a dissection ; but I never accepted his invitations, thinking that my nerves belonged to the living, not to the dead, and I had better finish my education as a nurse before I began that of a surgeon. But I never met the little man skipping through the hall, with oddly shaped cases in his hand, and an absorbed expression of countenance, without being sure that a select party of surgeons were at work in the dead house, which idea was a rather trying one, when I knew the subject was some person whom I had nursed and cared for.

But this must not lead any one to suppose that the surgeons were willfully hard or cruel, though one of them remorsefully confided to me that he feared his profession blunted his sensibilities, and, perhaps, rendered him indifferent to the sight of pain.

I am inclined to think that in some cases it does ; for, though a capital surgeon and a kindly man, Dr. P., through long acquaintance with many of the ills flesh is heir to, had acquired a somewhat trying habit of regarding a man and his wound as separate institutions, and seemed rather annoyed that the former should express any opinion upon the latter, or claim any right in it, while under his care. He had a way of twitching off a bandage, and giving a limb a comprehensive sort of clutch, which, though no doubt entirely scientific, was rather startling than soothing, and highly objectionable as a means of preparing nerves for any fresh trial. He also expected the patient to assist in small operations, as he considered them, and to restrain all demonstrations during the process.

"Here, my man, just hold it this way, while I look into it a bit," he said one day to Fitz G., putting a wounded arm into the keeping of a sound one, and proceeding to poke about among bits of bone and visible muscles, in a red and black chasm made by some infernal machine of the shot or shell description. Poor Fitz held on like grim Death, ashamed to show fear before a woman, till it grew more than he could bear in silence; and, after a few smothered groans, he looked at me imploringly, as if he said, ": I wouldn't, ma'am, if I could help it," and fainted quietly away.

Dr. P. looked up, gave a compassionate sort of cluck, and poked away more busily than ever, with a nod at me and a brief — "Never mind; be so good as to hold this till I finish."

I obeyed, cherishing the while a strong desire to insinuate a few of his own disagreeable knives and scissors into him, and see how he liked it. A very disrespectful and ridiculous fancy, of course; for he was doing all that could be done, and the arm prospered finely in his hands. But the human mind is prone to prejudice; and, though a personable man, speaking French like a born "Parley voo," and whipping off legs like an animated guillotine, I must confess to a sense of relief when he was ordered elsewhere; and suspect that several of the men would have faced a rebel battery with less trepidation than they did Dr. P., when he came briskly in on his morning round.

As if to give us the pleasures of contrast, Dr. Z. succeeded him, who, I think, suffered more in giving pain than did his patients in enduring it; for he often paused to ask: " Do I nurt you ?" and, seeing his solicitude, the boys invariably answered : " Not much ; go ahead, Doctor," though the lips that uttered this amiable fib might be white with pain as they spoke. Over the dressing of some of the wounds, we used to carry on conversations upon subjects foreign to the work in hand, that the patient might forget himself in the charms of our discourse. Christmas eve was spent in this way; the Doctor strapping the little Sergeant's arm, I holding the lamp, while all three laughed and talked, as if anywhere but in a hospital ward ; except when the chat was broken by a long-drawn " Oh ! " from " Baby B.," an abrupt request from the Doctor to " Hold the lamp a little higher, please," or an encouraging, " Most through, Sergeant," from Nurse P.

The chief Surgeon, Dr. O., I was told, refused the higher salary, greater honor, and less labor, of an appointment to the Officer's Hospital, round the corner, that he might serve the poor fellows at Hurlyburly House, or go to the front, working there day and night, among the horrors that succeed the glories of a battle. I liked that so much, that the quiet, brown-eyed Doctor was my especial admiration ; and when my own turn came, had more faith in him than in all the rest put together, although he did advise me to go home, and authorize the consumption of blue pills.

Speaking of the surgeons reminds me that, having found all manner of fault, it becomes me to celebrate the redeeming feature of Hurlyburly House. I had been prepared by the accounts of others, to expect much humiliation of spirit from the surgeons, and to be treated by them like a door-mat, a worm, or any other meek and lowly article, whose mission it is to be put down and walked upon ; nurses being considered as mere servants, receiving the lowest pay, and, it's my private opinion, doing the hardest work of any part of the army, except the mules. Great, therefore, was my surprise, when I found myself treated with the utmost courtesy and kindness. Very soon my carefully prepared meekness was laid upon the shelf; and, going from one extreme to the other, I more than once expressed a difference of opinion regarding sundry messes it was my painful duty to administer.

As eight of us nurses chanced to be off duty at once, we had an excellent opportunity of trying the virtues of these gentlemen; and I am bound to say they stood the test admirably, as far as my personal observation went. Dr. O.'s stethescope was unremitting in its attentions; Dr. S. brought his buttons into my room twice a day, with the regularity of a medical clock; while Dr. Z. filled my table with neat little bottles, which I never emptied, prescribed Browning, bedewed me with Cologne, and kept my fire going, as if, like the candles in St. Peter's, it must never be permitted to die out. Waking one cold night, with the certainty that my last spark had expired, and consequently hours of coughing were in store for me, I was much amazed to see a ruddy light dancing on the wall, a jolly blaze roaring up the chimney, and, down upon his knees before it, Dr. Z., whittling shavings. I ought to have risen up and thanked him on the spot; but, knowing that he was one of those who like to do good by stealth, I only peeped at him as if he were a friendly ghost; till, having made things as cozy as the most motherly of nurses could have done, he crept away, leaving me to feel, as somebody says, "as if angels were a watching of me in my sleep;" though that species of wild fowl do not usually descend in broadcloth and glasses. I afterwards discovered that he split the wood himself on that cool January midnight, and went about making or mending fires for the poor old ladies in their dismal dens; thus causing himself to be regarded as a bright and shining light in more ways than one. I never thanked him as I ought; therefore, I publicly make a note of it, and further aggravate that modest M. D. by saying that if this was not being the best of doctors and the gentlest of gentlemen, I shall be happy to see any improvement upon it.

To such as wish to know where these scenes took place, I must respectfully decline to answer; for Hurly-burly House has ceased to exist as a hospital; so let it rest, with all its sins upon its head, — perhaps I should say chimney top. When the nurses felt ill, the doctors departed, and the patients got well, I believe the concern gently faded from existence, or was merged into some other and better establishment, where I hope the washing of three hundred sick people is done out of the house, the food is eatable, and mortal women are not expected to possess an angelic exemption from all wants, and the endurance of truck horses.

Since the appearance of these hasty Sketches, I have heard from several of my comrades at the Hospital; and their approval assures me that I have not let sympathy and fancy run away with me, as that lively team is apt to do when harnessed to a pen. As no two persons see the same thing with the same eyes, my view of hospital life must be taken through my glass, and held for what it is worth. Certainly, nothing was set down in malice, and to the serious-minded party who objected to a tone of levity in some portions of the Sketches, I can only say that it is a part of my religion to look well after the cheerfulnesses of life, and let the dismals shift for themselves; believing, with good Sir Thomas More, that it is wise to " be merrie in God."

The next hospital I enter will, I hope, be one for the colored regiments, as they seem to be proving their right to